Fantastic FEEDER FISHING

by Archie Braddock

Edited by Colin Dyson

PUBLICATIONS

First published in 1992 by
Pisces Angling Publications
PO Box 657
Sheffield S10 1AT

British Library Cataloguing-in-Publication Data:
A catalogue record for this book is available from
the British Library

ISBN 0 948584 09 2

Drawings by PJC Graphics, Newark, Notts.

Typeset by Pisces Angling Publications

Printed in Great Britain by
Joseph Ward & Son
Dewsbury
West Yorks

Fantastic FEEDER FISHING

Archie Braddock

To Shirley

who makes it all possible

CONTENTS

FOREWORD
by Colin Dyson

Archie Braddock has been around a long time, and I guess our
friendship is now quite long-standing. I have tried to remember
when it began, but the memory fails. It undoubtedly sprang from my
Editorship of Coarse Angler magazine, but beyond that I cannot
recall. That's the trouble with fishing with Archie; the mind has to be
kept clear for the important things. There is no room left for the
trivia.

Fishing with him is not always a peaceful and totally relaxing
experience. One is bombarded with information - proven and
unproven theories, what he has been doing, where he has been fishing,
what he will be trying next, the latest step along the road to
understanding the complex business of bait ingredients, additives,
flavours, what works best for which of the species, and when...

It has been my fortune (or misfortune) to be pike fishing with Archie
during part of his learning process on feeder fishing, and almost
throughout the key period when he was making remarkable progress
with special baits. I may have managed to point him in the right
direction here and there on feeder techniques, but his knowledge on
baits is all his own, and quite phenomenal. I doubt there is anyone
outside the world of carp fishing who understands the subject more
thoroughly than he does, and he is probably light years in front of

those who have tried to apply such knowledge in the pursuit of species other than carp. It has enhanced his own fishing beyond all measure.

Many match and pleasure anglers are playing around with special baits, without appreciating what they are doing right - or wrong. Archie was in the same boat before he got around to studying the writings of all the acknowledged experts in carp fishing. He knows the areas where they agree, and where they differ. Privately, nowadays, he will pronounce on who is right and who is wrong in some key areas, but it was a long time before he became that confident. Throughout years of endless experiment he has written down everything he has tried, and evaluated the results. He knows what works and what doesn't, and for which species. He knows which of the many flavours work at different times of the season.

Using that information, and polishing his approach to feeder fishing to the point of perfection, has produced for him sport of a spectacular and very consistent standard. He catches when others don't, and that is surely the ultimate goal. When he reached it, and found himself with nowhere else to go, he suddenly announced that he was going to give it a rest, and intended to switch to a new challenge - catching a 30lb carp from the River Trent. His first fish of the 1991/2 season weighed 25lb 2oz, but that is not his best. The 30lb mark has already trembled - 29lb 4oz common a few weeks after the 25! - and knowing him as I do I am convinced he will succeed. Archie Braddock is relentlessly dedicated to that end, and that is enough for me!

He is one of the most ambitious and successful anglers I have ever met, and yet the chances are that you may not have heard of him. That is perhaps because he has not gone out of his way to court publicity, and he has certainly never been a "circuit angler." Not for him the wandering role to the going waters. He has concentrated on doing well on home territory, and good fish from local waters are every bit as hard to catch as monsters from places like Redmire.

Archie does not venture into print too often, but when he does it is always interesting. He may not be a household name, but rest assured that the big names know him well enough. He was sought out by John Bailey, when he was putting together his excellent book "The Great Anglers," and more recently Rod Hutchinson looked him up for a contribution to his book on the early days of carp fishing. Well, I did say that he went back a long way!

He caught his first double figure carp, 10lb 10oz, at the age of 20 - the year Dick Walker caught his 44-pounder. He invented the

anchored crust method of carp fishing, and caught a Mapperley carp of
16lb in 1960. Only the early pioneers of the game will know how
difficult that was. A January 21-pounder in the mid-1960s was a
headline maker in that era, and when Dick Walker first publicised
Betalight fishing in the '70s Archie had been using them for quite some
time.

He was effective enough as a carp pioneer to become one of the first
victims of jealous reaction - as sincere a form of flattery as imitation
ever was. It was the same when he pioneered barbel fishing on
Derbyshire's River Dove. The unsuccessful conspired to get him
banned, but he just turned his attention to something else. There is
always a challenge facing Archie Braddock!

It was Archie who re-discovered the Trent barbel in 1973. He was
possibly the first to use pop-up baits for pike, and he devised the
deadliest deadbaiting rig for pike that I have ever used. In a
roundabout way I suppose I am trying to convey that Archie is an all-
rounder, who just happens to be writing about feeder fishing in this
book. That he is doing so is my responsibility. When he first told me he
was switching to Trent carp he had remarked, without false modesty,
that he had nothing left to learn.

"Then why don't you write a book on it?" I asked. "Nobody has
tackled specialist legering properly since Peter Stone, a good many
years ago now. There is nothing comprehensive on the feeder, and
absolutely nothing at all on the bait technology you have spent so
much time researching."

"OK," he said. "I'll write it if you will publish it." So that is why we
are here. Having read my way avidly through Archie's manuscript I
have the feeling that even the experienced match enthusiasts will find
much to learn from him. Indeed, Archie doesn't mince his words on
the subject of match anglers. He thinks some of their techniques are
plain wrong, and believes they could all improve their catches if they
knew what he can teach them about baits.

That subject is complex, or ends up looking that way whenever
anyone tries to explain it, but he leads the reader gently into it,
explaining what everything is and what it does before becoming more
and more advanced. I understand it a lot better myself now, thanks to
him, and have derived much personal benefit from his work. I am sure
that you will, too.

The final dimension of this book is that he tackles what is probably
the last frontier in carp fishing. There has been no authoritative

account of river carping, as far as I know, but Archie has managed to achieve instant success on the Trent by adapting his feeder fishing approach and applying what he has learned about baits. Carp enthusiasts who are bored with the pursuit of known, named fish in stillwaters, are beginning to realise that the Trent offers them the opportunity to explore the unknown. Nobody knows what the potential is, but there are anglers who have landed, without much difficulty, 30s and late 20s, and who will speak in hushed tones about fish they have been completely unable to control. Archie tangled with several, and assumed that this was what fit 20lb commons in flowing water were like. But then he started catching low and high 20s, and began to wonder what the hell he had been battling with before! His accounts of his lost battles in the carp chapter are mind-blowing!

As you will have gathered I am enthusiastic about this book. The one area in which I am less so concerns the photographs, some of them anyway. His picture collection is not that of a man who intended to publish a book one day. It is the collection of one who so often fishes alone, and packs up in the dark. He will not sack up big fish for the sake of perfect pictures in the middle of next morning, nor will he even bother to try and photograph big catches of fish.

His pictures are mainly those of an angler who puts the fish first; the quick snaps of a man who thought he just needed something for a private record. Some are good; others not so good, but I have used them anyway. They help to tell a tale, and to prove what he is preaching.

A work or art it ain't, nor was it ever intended to be. What It is, though, is a book which is almost unique in the breadth of its appeal. Anyone who fishes the feeder, match or pleasure fisherman, can learn from it. Everyone can benefit from Archie's knowledge of baits, perhaps even some of the carp anglers, who will certainly be interested in his approach to the monsters of the River Trent.

INTRODUCTION

by Archie Braddock

It was in the late 1970s when I first became interested in feeder
fishing, and that interest has grown steadily over the years. I regard
it nowadays as a skill equal to to the art of stick float and waggler
fishing - approaches with which the real experts expect to hit just
about every bite.

It was Benny Ashurst, I believe, who coined the immortal expression
that "legering was in its infantry" (his malapropism, not mine!),
coupling it with the opinion that a fortune awaited the man who could
learn to hit every bite on the leger. Well, I think we have reached that
stage now, certainly in a number of feeder fishing situations. If you get
it right the results can be fantastic; there is no other word to describe it.
Let me give you a few examples...

*River Trent, February: From dawn to dusk, for more than nine hours,
the fish came in steady procession. Bream between 3lb 8oz and 4lb
8oz, quality roach to 1lb 4oz, chub from 2lb 8oz to 3lb 8oz, perch to
2lb 12oz, even gudgeon. The only interruption to this regular run of
fish was a near half-hour battle with a 14lb 12oz common carp. With
frost biting hard after sunset I released the fifth and last load from my
big keepnet. I estimated the total weight to be in excess of 150lb, but
was really too tired to care...*

*Midlands Reservoir, August: It's a lovely, warm evening and quality
bream follow one after the other, giving me no time to re-cast the
second rod, which is thrown up the bank behind me. After seven fish I
no longer put them in the net, for I won't risk over-crowding just for*

the sake of a trophy-type photograph. After about five hours of it I give up, and weigh the seven fish in the net - 5lb 3oz, 5lb 5oz, two at 5lb 8oz, 5lb 10oz, 5lb 12oz and 5lb 13oz. All the others were about the same...

Trent backwater, December: A sudden thaw has pushed the river to the top of its banks, a surging grey-green gush of melted snow. The water temperature is 39 degrees F. - a drastic drop for this power station-warmed river, which often runs above 50 degrees F., even in winter. The few anglers who are around report only the odd tiny fish, or just maggots with the ends nipped. Typical snow-water results. I drop a feeder in the edge of the main flow, and the first bite comes in about a minute - a sudden, fast pull on the quiver. Ten seconds later it comes again, bouncing the quivertip with gusto. The line drops slack as the vigorous bite drags the feeder out of place, and I wind in to find a well-hooked 4oz roach attached. This continues steadily for about three hours, with roach, gudgeon, hybrids and small bream to 1lb. Intermittent rain becomes continuous, so I pack up. The other anglers are long gone... Why did those fish feed for me, and nobody else? Luck? or was it the bait..?

These are just random samples, taken from many hundreds of similar sessions. When I go feeder fishing I expect to catch a lot of fish, including some of the bigger ones, and I expect them to start feeding soon after starting to fish. If they don't I am doing something wrong. It all sounds incredible, doesn't it? But no, I am not some super angler. My basic skills are probably inferior to those of the average matchman's, but I score in other ways!

I have put a great deal of time and thought into what I do, and have experimented endlessly to establish what I now consider to be the perfect approach on all kinds of different waters. It has given me the best sport any angler could wish for, and it is not beyond the capacity of anyone to do the same.

This book is a record of how I have reached my present standard. It is a record of how I evolved the baits and rigs which now give me the sort of fishing I once could only dream about.

Footnote: I have no financial connection with any tackle manufacturer or bait supplier, in this country or elsewhere. When I mention anything by trade name it is solely because I use it, and it works.

LONG RANGE
FEEDER

Way back in 1959 I spent a week in Ireland, at a town called Ballinamore, in County Leitrim, almost on the shores of the vast Lough Garadice. I had spent most of the week fishing the lough, catching lots of bream on legered lobworms. Easy fishing, nice deep water at close range, no problems... In fact it was so easy I decided to fish the All Ireland match, which was to be held on the water on the coming weekend. With six hundred anglers and a huge cash prize, and me with a week of practice under my belt, I figured I was in with a chance.

The match was split into six sections, and my draw put me on the far side of the lough, which I hadn't seen before. When I got there the sun was beating down, and my heart sank. I could see the rocky bottom all the way out; it was only about a foot deep! The eventual winner and all the first dozen came from the deep shore, but I won my hundred-peg section easily. I had the ultimate long range gear for that period - Mark IV split cane Avon rod, a Mitchell reel and a tin of the "new" streamlined Arlesey bombs, which Richard Walker had just invented. I could out-cast everyone else and reach water which was a bit deeper, picking up a few 3lb bream.

That was a valuable lesson to learn at that stage of my career. Whether you are a pleasure fisherman, a matchman or a specialist the ability to fish well at long range can give you a great advantage, but to a significant extent that ability has been lost by many anglers today. They are inhibited by modern tackle, strange though that may sound, but it will become clear what I mean in a while.

My introduction to serious long-range feeder fishing came at Clumber Park Lake in the 1970s. For those who do not know it, Clumber is a large estate lake, very shallow over most of its area. It is fed by a stream and was, and still is, a very rich water, full of weed in the summer. Most of this dies away in the winter, leaving a clean gravel bottom, and that was when I used to fish it. The main species were roach, which ran very large indeed, and bream, which were also big by the standards of the time. Roach to 2lb 14oz and bream to 9lb were the biggest taken while I fished there, so I was obviously keen to sort it out. Clumber is day tickets on the bank, and is consequently hard-fished. With much of the water 2ft. 6in. deep or less, and very clear, the fish are understandably cautious. They keep well away from the banks, staying in the deepest area, which is probably about 4ft. 6in. deep.

With overhanging trees everywhere the overhead casting was somewhat restricted, and a cast of around 60 yards was required to reach the best spots. To complicate the job even further the prevailing winds were usually facers, though I liked it to be windy. The fish very definitely fed best in a good blow, so I didn't mind having to cope with it.

I bought a pair of soft-actioned Conoflex glass rods, 1lb 4oz test curve and 11ft. 3in. long. They were matched up with Mitchell 410 reels filled with 3lb line, and proved to be just right for the job. The feeders I chose were Drennan feeder-links, block end jobs which are still available in most tackle shops. With a long, streamlined body with the reel line running through the centre, and all the lead at one end, it

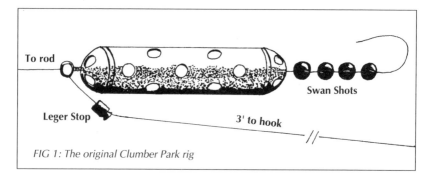

FIG 1: The original Clumber Park rig

Clumber
Park lake,
viewed
from the
dam wall

was the best available long-range feeder on the market. My first set-up looked like this (Fig 1). With maggots as bait I started to catch a few roach, good fish up to 1lb plus, but I just wasn't able to reach the fish on the windier days.

The first modification was to dispense with the swanshots and tie on a half ounce bomb, which greatly enhanced the casting efficiency, but now the hook link was prone to catching around the bomb. After a lot of thought I drilled out the nose cone of the feeder and pushed the swivel of the bomb inside, sealing it in place with Araldite adhesive. While doing this I streamlined the bomb by smoothing the glue into the area around the nose of the feeder, leaving no little awkward places for the hooklink to catch in. At the same time I carried out some further small modifications.

All the feederlinks are made from plastic which is just too thin, and the feeder would start to break up during the first session, under the impact of the splashdown. I also found that the top end cap soon began to work loose, spilling out the maggots in flight. To conquer that I put a strip of insulating tape around the feeder at the cap end, to reinforce it, and I also put a leger-stop on the link between the feeder and the brass ring. This was slid down to the cap after filling the feeder, holding it securely in position. It worked extremely well, the tape holding the feeder together for a lot longer than the original product, and no more maggot spillages. The finished item looked like this (Fig 2). Now I had me a missile! With these feeders I could reach the fish against almost any wind; they really did cast like a dream. I still have them today, and would not hesitate to use them whenever maximum range is required.

Of course fishing in excess of 60 yards on a shallow water does bring with it a whole new set of problems, not the least of which is bite indication. It is here that I start to part company with the thinking of the present-day match anglers, mostly on the tackle they use for the job. We invariably see them, and most pleasure anglers for that matter, trying to fish at long range with quivertips and swingtips. Now these are fine for registering bites, but that facility is useless if the rod cannot cast the required distance. Very powerful heavy feeder tip rods might make the distance, but they would not be too good at bite registration, would they?

It follows that the need is for a rod which can cast the distance, and

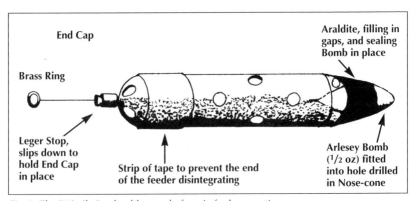

Fig. 2: The "Missile," a durable, tangle-free rig for long casting

a sensitive bite indication system, but what? At long range, and arguably for shorter range as well, the best choice is a butt indicator, of the type which clips to the line between the first and second rings. It is anchored to the front rod rest by a length of strong line or cord. They are generally known as bobbins, and can be bought over the counter in most tackle shops. There are some incorporating Betalights for use at night, so if you do any after dark fishing it is best to opt for them.

The bobbin method was fine for Clumber, but I soon found the main drawback was line drag - not surprising when one considers the vast amount of line in the water. All large stillwaters produce strong undertows in windy conditions, and the shallower the water the greater is the effect. Add the problem of Clumber's feeder stream flowing through the lake, and the effect was to see the bobbin sliding smoothly up to jam in the rod ring in perfect imitation of a good bite. There is, of course, a way around it. Just insert a length of strong line between the retaining cord and the bobbin, and pinch enough swanshots onto it to counter-balance the drag. On the wildest days I have had as many as seven swanshots on the link and when you consider that eight swanshots = half an ounce that is some undertow! Do not, however, imagine that it is insensitive. The weight is only just countering the undertow, and the slightest change in pressure, increase or decrease, will immediately register as a bite as the indicator lifts or falls. The set-up is illustrated in Fig. 3 (next page). The bite indication was nearly always the same - a half inch twitch, nothing more. An instant strike was needed at Clumber, or the result would be just crushed maggots.

Another problem was the natural preference of the roach to wait until the falling light before they would feed. Imagine the scene. An icy wind is roaring down a hundred acres of water, straight into the face, and the temperature falls even lower as the light fades. You try to ignore it, peering through watering eyes for that little twitch on the indicator, knowing that despite the numbness you must leap into instant action when it moves. I well remember sitting there on such a night with that well-known big fish man Dave Plummer. We hadn't had a bite, and each of us was trying to show how tough we were by ignoring the bitter conditions. Suppressing a shiver, and trying to sound casual, I said: "You know, Dave, it could get cold tonight." As the gale ripped around us he replied: "I hope it doesn't get windy with it."

Despite the occasional privations I had some wonderful roach fishing at Clumber. I had my first 2-pounder there, with four others of 1lb 12oz or more in the same short, four hour session. That's about as long

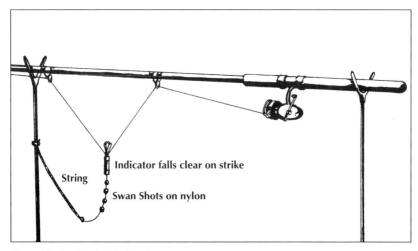

Fig. 3: The bobbin bite indication system

as I could stay hyped up enough to hit those mini-bites, which rarely exceeded two an hour. In the search for more I tried changing from 3lb line and a 14 spade end hook baited with two maggots to a 20 on a 1.5lb bottom and a single maggot. It made no difference at all, so I went heavier - 5lb line, 10 hook and four maggots, with a threequarter ounce bomb in the feeder. Surprising though it may seem to those indoctrinated in the "light fantastic" school of angling this in fact improved the results, though only slightly. I think the main reason it worked was that I could cast a bit further with the heavier tackle. I tried moving around the lake, which is shaped like an elongated triangle, but I established that there was a very definite pecking order among the roach. The biggest fish inhabited the deepest water, at the base of the triangle. Some 200 yards up the lake there were far more fish, but most of them were around the 1lb mark. Higher up still there were loads of fish, but not many as big as one pound.

So it had to be back to base camp, facing the weather. By switching to a Betalight bobbin I managed to avoid the eye strain brought on by the dusk, and I also fished on into the dark several times. This taught me a great deal. I found that roach, bream and even eels would feed several hours after dark on the coldest winter night, and in very shallow water. One February night the water actually froze up around my tackle, and my casts got shorter and shorter as the ice closed in around me. But I still continued to get bites, even when I could drop into only two feet of rapidly freezing water. I finally had to stop when

A 2lb 2oz roach from the lake at Clumber Park

my feeder stopped splashing and started skidding instead! Great days, good fish, and invaluable knowledge gained.

Clumber was to suffer a few problems, including a near complete drain down. Some fool began to lower the lake for work to be carried out on the dam wall, and forgot to close the sluice. It was almost totally dry, with most of the fish tobogganing into the stream below the outfall, but it recovered far more quickly than most had imagined. Not long ago I decided to give it another try for old times' sake. I arrived at around 10 a.m. on a weekday, but there wasn't a swim to be had within 400 yards of the dam wall. After dark fishing had been stopped, thanks to the behaviour of the idiot minority, and I didn't stay long. I managed to catch a roach of 1lb 8oz by making really long casts from an unfavoured swim, but my heart wasn't in it. Fishing is like life. You should never go back.

Reservoir bream and roach

About ten years after the heights of the Clumber fishing I found myself on the banks of a huge Midlands reservoir, nearly 200 acres of mostly deep water. Due to its size and volume it was not an easy place to fish, but the locals had assured me it held "lots of 2lb roach." Furthermore practically all the tench were "over 6lb," and the bream were "great slabs of 7lb or more."

The trip was timed to coincide with a small match of 20 pegs, one of the few to be held there. All the anglers were using the feeder, almost all of them on the block end, and it was a fine August afternoon. Nineteen of them blanked completely, and the winner had a bag of 11 bream between four and six pounds, plus a "2lb roach" which actually weighed 1lb 8oz. These anglers do not lie deliberately. They spend so much of their time catching little roach that anything much over 1lb looks colossal, and they have nothing to judge it by. Their stories of "twos" are related to the bailiff, repeated in the pubs and tackle shops, and legends are born!

The winner had been using an open ended feeder (he was the only one who had, in fact), plugged with groundbait, with a single maggot on a 1.1lb line to a 22 hook. As a result he had to spend four or five minutes landing every fish, and he broke off on three of them. He could have doubled his catch by using heavier tackle, by landing them sooner and not cracking off, but of course he was a victim of the angling Press. We regularly see articles by so-called experts claiming that hook sizes of 22, 24 or even 26 are necessary. They start with a 1.1lb line and go down to, perhaps, 12oz line.

As a result of this many average anglers will now commence their days' fishing with ultra fine tackle, without stopping to consider whether it is really needed. The inevitable result is breakage, and fish are left with hooks and line trailing from their mouths. You see these stories every week in match reports. Joe Bloggs wins his Christmas fur and feather with 27lb of chub, and "would have had a lot more if he hadn't lost seven fish in a snag!" If I break off once I am concerned; obviously I have done something wrong, or it wouldn't have happened.

I will use finer lines for float fishing, but for more than a decade now I have never used a hook link of less than 3lb BS while feeder fishing. I have fished hard waters like Clumber, and even harder-fished rivers, like the Trent, where so many of these light tackle stories emanate from. I have not felt at a disadvantage with stronger tackle than they advocate. Get the rest of it right and ultra fine tackle is not necessary, so read on...

Our reservoir match winner had made his catch about 40 yards out, which was about as far as his light quivertip rod could manage, yet he was still getting 10 yards beyond everyone else. This was one of the main reasons why he caught and they didn't; the other reason was his choice of an open-ended feeder. This is a major factor in successful feeder fishing, as it can be used to deposit sweetcorn and all manner of other baits which I will come to later. Of equal importance are the plugs of groundbait used to block the feeder, as scores of different additives and flavours can be added to them to improve the attraction. I go into this in great depth in a later chapter.

Also extremely important is the set-up of the terminal tackle, and I expect you all have your own ideas on this subject. After many years of experimentation, during which I have tried every rig that has ever been publicised (and a few which haven't) I have no hesitation in saying which is best - the fixed paternoster with a short lead/feeder link and a long hook link is by far the most successful. I know I am at odds with some in the match fishing game, but they are deluding themselves.

Now and again the leading lights will publish wonderful looking rigs involving one or more loops and a sliding feeder, but there is one inescapable fact about these and other "running rigs." Unless you are fishing at short range, with the biting fish moving directly away from you, running rigs do not run! What happens is either the feeder moves or the line goes through the swivel or loop in a series of small jerks, clearly signalled by the twitching quivertip or butt indicator. Either way it can mean a rapidly ejected bait. Fixed paternoster bites are much more positive, and easier to strike.

My own set-up, which I use for 95% of my feeder fishing, is shown in Fig. 4 (next page). Although it seems basically simple every item is vital. The snap link is simply there so I can change quickly to a different size of feeder. The Drennan ring on the feeder itself makes a quick change that much easier, and the silicon rubber protects what is a potential tangle point. The other Drennan ring is a joining point for the three separate lines. It may look flimsy for the heavier feeders, but it is incredibly strong. Let me tell you how strong. While carp fishing on the Trent, with 15lb line, I hooked a double bed mattress, which was lying on the bottom 30 yards out. With a massive pull I got it moving, but it swung round and downstream. I then managed to pull it

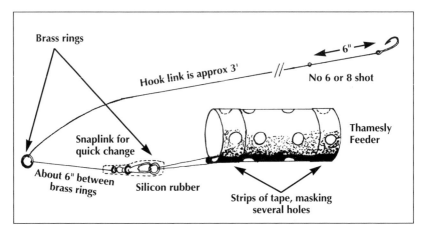

Fig. 4: The fixed paternoster feeder rig.

up against the current to the bank, where it proved physically impossible to drag out. The little brass ring in my set-up wasn't even distorted.

The strips of tape cover most of the holes in the feeder, as I want my feed emerging around the hook-bait, not flying out on the cast, crashing out on splashdown or dribbling out as the feeder sinks. The common and often repeated advice to "open up the holes to let the maggots out quicker" appears totally self-defeating to me. I can put all mine exactly where I want them by making a few false strikes to empty the feeder, and then rapidly re-casting. The reason I do not block all the holes is that I need water to seep in behind the plugs of groundbait, to help them disperse.

The shot is very significant, for it greatly assists the prevention of tangles, particularly when casting into a facing wind. It also prevents the baited hook flopping in a heap on top of the feeder as it sinks in deep water. Imagine the tackle sinking with and without a shot, and you will see what I mean. The shot size can vary from a swan to a dust, but in long range fishing it is usually a no. 6 or 8.

Several years ago I tried to get the best of both worlds by using a 6in. feeder link, free-running on the main line and stopped by a leger stop 3ft. from the hook. I was catching plenty of fish, but suddenly developed a tangle which locked everything solid at the leger stop. I couldn't be bothered to re-tackle, and just carried on fishing with what was then a fixed paternoster rig.

I caught just as many fish as before and the bites were better, thus settling the question of which was the most efficient rig.

A bite on this rig slackens the link line between the feeder and the main line, effectively by-passing the feeder. This means the only objects between the fish and the butt indicator are a small shot and a small brass ring, which makes the set-up very sensitive indeed. If a very fast bite occurs the fish moves the ring from A to B, hitting the feeder. This means the fish usually hooks itself, rather like the bolt rig principle in carp fishing (See Figs. 5a and 5b, below).

If the fish moves towards the rod the feeder will move and the indicator drops back. For that reason I always set the indicator hanging forwards of centre, and add one or two swanshots to the indicator even when there is no undertow. I also reduce the feeder weight to the lowest possible weight which can be cast to the required distance. The weight of the contents will generally supply any extra punch which is needed.

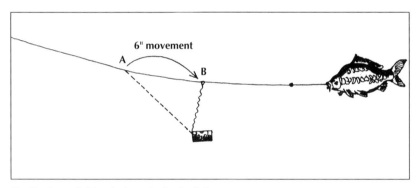

Fig. 5a: A steady bite slackens the feeder link.

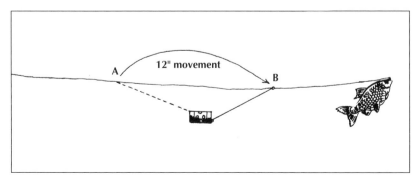

Fig. 5b: A fast bite hits the feeder.

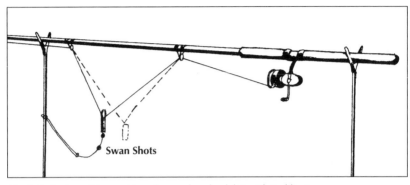

Fig. 6: Indicator set forward to enhance drop-back bites (dotted line).

This arrangement "spring loads the whole rig, for the slightest pull by the fish towards the angler causes the indicator to fall back very fast, magnifying the bite. The diagram shows this (Fig. 6).

The feeders I use are the open-ended types made by Thamesly in three sizes, and I choose the middle-sized one most of the time. It is about 2.5 inches long, made of strong green plastic, and carries .75oz of lead as bought. This is often more than is needed, so I prise it off and replace it with a lighter strip to enhance those drop-back bites. If no suitable lead is available I buy the cheapest feeders I can find and dump them after stripping the leads off. I then add another small piece of lead to the Thamesly by Aralditing a half inch strip to the front end (Fig 7). This gives me a weight-forward feeder which will out-cast a normal feeder every time. It is more stable in flight, because it doesn't wobble about so much, and it is more accurate and less prone to tangles. It's a small alteration which achieves a great improvement.

In long-range feeder fishing line diameter can have a significant

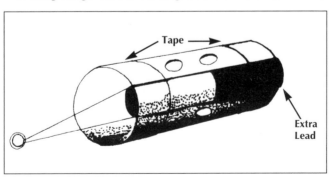

Fig. 7: Extra lead glued to the feeder enhances long casting

effect, and I spent a lot of time trying the different brands before I settled on Bayer Ultima. The 6.5lb has a lower diameter than every other 6lb on the market, and has a smooth, hard finish. It literally hisses through the rings while other stuff just clatters. More important still it can stand up to full-blooded casts with loaded feeders weighing an ounce or more, and keep it up for weeks on end with no loss of strength. Recently Bayer down-rated all these lines, so the spool now reads 5.5lb BS. I now buy it by diameter measurement, in this case .020mm, which is shown on the spool.

Hook links can be any strength you wish, and I use the Ultima 3.6lb, 4.6lb and 6.5lb, with size 14, 12 and 10 hooks, and whichever combination has been chosen it has made very little difference to my catches. Nowadays I have about a dozen 4ft hook links of varying strengths, shot already on, stored on small pole winders. If you have to tie on a new one valuable time can be lost making them up on the bank, in the middle of a feeding spell.

I was equipped as described when, the day after that match I watched, I arrived at the reservoir in the late afternoon. I also had Optonic bite alarms on the front rod rests. For those not familiar with them just ask in your local tackle shop, where they will be happy to demonstrate one. I use them all the time, for they sound off just as well to a drop-back bite as they do to a straight pull. They take the strain out of a slow session, enabling you to watch the water for rolling fish, the bird life and the bathing beauties (if any) while waiting for the bites.

Before tackling up I spent half an hour casting a Depthometer around. This marvellous little gadget is a plastic tube, with a scale on it marking the depth in feet. It's a bit like the body of a hypodermic needle. It measures up to 100ft, but is not all that accurate below five feet. You tie it on the line, cast it out and let it sink to the bottom. Water enters through a small hole, and the deeper it goes the more water is forced in. When you wind it in and hold it upright the depth is registered on the gauge by the amount of water inside. It is an absolutely invaluable gadget for any angler, but not one in a thousand has one. (See Fig 8). They can be bought by mail order, from The Tackle Shop, Bridge Road,

Fig. 8: The Depthometer, an invaluable gadget for the specialist angler.

Gainsborough, Lincs. On many waters it has helped me to find a feature, a shallower area surrounded by deeper water, or a sudden increase in depth, but here I found only a steady shelve down, the further out I went. I had spotted the odd good roach topping in the waves about 60 to 70 yards out, where the depth was about 17ft. One difficulty with casting to such ranges with the sun in your eyes and a ripple on the water is being sure you have reached the same distance every time. This can easily be settled by casting to where you want to fish, and letting the feeder sink on an open bail arm. As soon as it hits bottom, and line ceases to peel from the spool, put a fairly tight elastic band over the remaining line on the spool. When you wind in the band will disappear under the coils, but every time you cast it will stop the feeder at the same distance. Should you hook a fish at maximum range which speeds off away from you, line will pull from under the band. If you pick out a tree, or some other feature on the far bank, as a casting marker, you will be sure of the right direction, as well as the distance. Having sorted all that out I settled down to fish, at first re-casting both rods (I always use two) every few minutes to get a layer of grub out there. Each rod had been cast at different ranges and different angles, so I was in fact fishing two separate swims. A word about two rod fishing. Do not put them out either side of you, or your head will be swivelling around like a spectator at Wimbledon. Put them close together on the right hand side, if you are right-handed, and then plant a third rod rest directly in front of you. You will find how useful this is the first time your near rod signals a fast bite while you are half way through filling a feeder for your far rod (Fig 9).

My baits were two fruit-flavoured maggots on a 14 eyed, round-bend hook, and the same flavour was used to mix the groundbait, with flavoured maggots in the feeder. Now I had done all I could think of to improve my chances, and I settled back into my folding chair to enjoy the warm summer evening. Out on the water the coots made their way busily back and forth; a pair of great crested grebes dived endlessly in an attempt to satiate the appetites of their squeaking offspring; and up in the air three terns were putting on a fantastic aerobatic display.

The reeds to one side, and the brambles behind me, were hives of activity. Butterflies, day-flying moths and bees of all sizes worked diligently for pollen, skilfully avoiding the multi-coloured spiders which lay in wait. The undergrowth around rustled with voles, which were hoping to get their heads in my groundbait bucket. There are many anglers I know who just are not interested in these things, and I have to admit that I too can become as intense as anyone else, but if ever I stop seeing what is happening around me I will probably give up fishing.

I had an hour in which to notice my surroundings before one of my indicators rose smoothly to the rod ring, and I struck into my first fish. A strong fight on a 3.6lb hook link produced a fine tench of 4lb 10oz, a good start. I was later to learn it was one of the 'sixes' the locals were always talking about. I weighed several 'six' and 'seven' pounders for proud captors over the next couple of years; they were all between 4lb 8oz and 4lb 15oz. I never once saw a genuine 5-pounder.

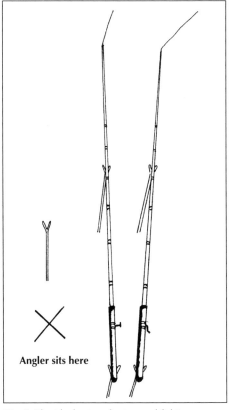

Fig. 9: The ideal set-up for two rod fishing.

This didn't matter, for it was the roach I really wanted. I ended that first session with two, weighing 1lb 1oz and 1lb 2oz, and they were gorgeous bars of silver. I have never seen such beautiful roach as those from that reservoir. They were fin and scale perfect, and had probably never seen a hook before. This is one of the benefits of long range fishing - you get among fish the others just can't reach, as the lager ad. says.

I fished that reservoir extensively for around three years, and learned a lot about deep water fishing. It was rare to fish at less than 12ft, and at times I was in as much as 22ft. As with almost all still waters a windy, cloudy day was best, and a flat calm usually meant no bites until near sunset. On the rougher evenings the roach showed a tendency to drift nearer the bank as it got closer to dusk, and this enabled me to use the Whopper Dropper. These huge bait droppers

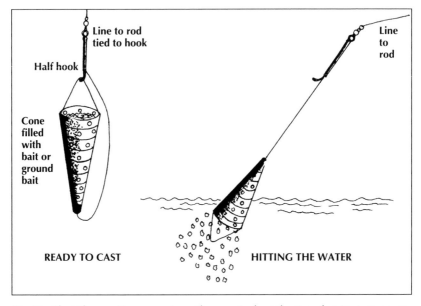

Fig. 10: The Whopper Dropper system. The cone is about the size of an ice-cream cone, with a wire handle at the wide end and strong line to a half hook running from the thin end. The hook, on a split ring, is tied to a spare rod. When the dropper is loaded the handle goes on the hook for casting. It detaches itself in flight, turns over and lands wide end first. It can be used to scatter loose feed, or to take feed to the bottom if plugged with groundbait.

can be had from the tackle companies which specialise in carp fishing products, and Fig. 10 explains how they work. When using two rods I tend to cast around with one of them if things are slow, searching for the fish. If I find them at 50 yards or less I bring the Whopper Dropper into play.

A word of warning. They carry a large amount of bait, plus a damp groundbait plug, which easily means you can be casting six ounces. This needs a heavy pike rod and 12lb line, which I always have with me just in case. It is the most effective way I know of getting a lot of feed down fast, for only six casts can really lay the table. From then on the usual feeder full should keep the swim topped up.

On the flat calm evenings with a clear sky I often went almost biteless until sunset, and the best I could hope for was perhaps an hour's feeding spell producing four or five fish. Casters would often prove far superior in these conditions, which set me thinking. Was it the extra buoyancy of this bait which attracted the fish? After all, on such days it was common to see lots of fish rolling at long range, and although I could reach them I was always conscious that my baited hook would be lying perhaps 18 feet below them. I started experimenting with floating maggots, and for those who are unfamiliar with how to do this you simply put a few hook maggots in a small container, along with a small amount of water; no more than enough to come half way up their bodies as they wriggle around in it. This does make them float, but the hook has to be very small and the line extremely fine, or the combined weight will make them sink again. Experiments in the margins showed the maggots off bottom all right, but if there was any undertow at all I imagined them leaning away from the feeder rather than rising well above it.

I did catch a few fish like this, but have to admit that I did not really follow through on it, mainly because I tended not to bother going to the reservoir if the conditions were calm. In retrospect I probably missed out. In more recent years I have found that adding regular Sense Appeal (of which more later) makes maggots float, and with the addition of a small piece of cork to the hook link, about a foot from the bait, it is possible to present maggots several feet above the feeder. You might like to try it.

I caught a lot of bream from that water, and when they really came on the feed one rod was as much as I could handle. Many was the time when the indicator was pulled from my fingers as I was trying to set it on the line, and this would go on for hour after hour. I never tried to fish through the night on one of these feeding spells as, frankly, it became too easy. After the first dozen fish it all becomes mechanical; casting out and reeling in 5lb to 5lb 8oz lumps which don't fight.

They were absolute suckers for fruity, sweet or creamy flavours, fished well out in deep water. I once found them spawning in the reservoir margins, and was staggered by their numbers. Along more than a quarter of a mile of bank, from under my feet to as far out as I could see with polaroid glasses, it was a heaving, jostling mass of bream. Thousands and thousands of them, all between four and six pounds. Really, there is no need to go to Ireland, once you have got your feeder fishing sorted out...

You may be thinking what I was, at the time - that I had perhaps become a one water man, and that just maybe it would be different somewhere else. With that in mind I took myself off to Mapperley Reservoir, in Derbyshire. It is only about 30 acres, barely an eighth of the size of the water I had been concentrating on, and a lot of it is 11

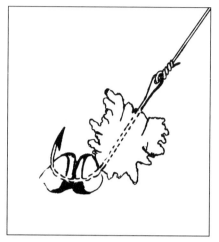

Fig. 11: Flake and sweetcorn on a long-shanked nymph hook.

to 12ft deep. It is also close to a heavily built-up area, and it is day ticket. That means it gets an awful lot of pressure, much of the time from feeder anglers, due to the depth.

I need not have worried. Even with 3lb hook links and an eyed 14 hook, fishing from tea time to dusk, I had half a dozen bream over 4lb, plus a few skimmers and roach, and I hadn't fished the water for 10 years. Apart from the right rig, plus flavours and additives (I used the fruity approach) the main factor was my distance casting. I was easily able to reach the middle of the water, which is where the fish were. So often I have found this with bream, particularly on the heavily fished waters. They just don't come near the banks until after dark. If I ever became a match fisherman I would book into such venues, knowing I would be in with a real chance.

On my big water I did not catch many tench, mainly, I think, because these fish roam much closer to the margins, so I was usually over-casting them. I spent a while fishing one rod at close range, but found a layer of silkweed in the shallower water, which made maggot fishing virtually useless. I tried sweetcorn, then bread flake, but found the best bait was a combination of both. I bought some long-shanked nymph hooks, as used in fly fishing, which gave me room to put two grains of corn on the bend of the hook, and a knob of flake on the shank (See Fig 11). The feeder was filled with corn and plugged with mashed bread, to which the juice of the corn had been added. This gave me one, maybe two tench, every time I tried it. None were less than 4lb, none more than 5lb, but every fish was a real scrapper. It also surprised me how often good roach picked up the bait, most of them over 1lb 8oz.

I also used caged feeders with this bait, sometimes, filled with pure white groundbait, as I have on occasion seen tench swimming quite quickly, well off the bottom. In clear water that blob of white will often pull down a cruising fish to investigate. I have caught the odd tench like this, but I suspect it could be vastly improved. I fancy using groundbait like "Explosive," and with a drier mix in the middle of the feeder and damper end plugs it ought to be possible to have a stream of flavoured particles dribbling upwards towards the surface. Again it is something I mean to do, but life is too short.

One August evening I learned a real lesson about the pulling power of flavoured maggots, when I stayed on into the dark for an hour. I found myself attached to something which ploughed heavily up and down for twenty minutes, ignoring my 3lb hook link and the pressure which came with it. With aching arms I finally netted a bulky shape, and caught a glimpse of a huge, rounded dorsal. My heart missed a beat. Had I caught the record tench? No, it was a pike of 17lbs, hooked cleanly in the jaw! It hadn't taken a small fish which had, in turn, taken my bait. And no, it wasn't a fluke.

Later that same season I hooked an even larger pike, which broke away after a long fight. The following year I caught yet another of 17lb 8oz, which, like the others, had picked up maggots, in the dark, in depths of 15ft and more. The only way they could have detected them is by smell, so they had obviously homed in on the flavours I was using. In later years I was to catch several more pike on flavoured maggots from other waters, though I would not suggest that feeder maggots are a viable method for the predators. Having learned, however, that pike are attracted to flavours, just like other fish, I put this to good use with flavoured sea fish deadbaits, on both rivers and stillwaters, in the following seasons.

Pike, tench, bream... I enjoyed them all, but it was the roach I really wanted, and I experimented endlessly with additives and flavourings, both in the groundbait and on the maggots. The results of this are included in the section on flavours, but it was sometimes quite remarkable how the roach preferred one taste on one trip, and another and different one the next time out. As the season advanced their tastes would change yet again as the water cooled. Far from being finnicky they became progressively easier to catch as I learned more, so I increased my tackle strength to cope with the tench and the occasional pike, without affecting my results with roach. My most successful rig included a no. 12 round bend eyed hook with four maggots, fished on 4.6lb Ultima. I even tried 6lb line to a no. 10 with six maggots, and even that didn't slow them down very much. They wanted the bait. The method was immaterial.

For around three years I plugged away at those roach, taking more than a hundred each season which weighed over 1lb. I never had a 'two,' although I did land many between 1lb 12oz and 1lb 15oz. One catch which will stay for ever in my memory came on the opening evening of the 1987 season. In four hours I caught 11 roach, but when I weighed these identical looking fish I could find a smallest of 1lb 9oz and a largest of 1lb 10oz. What a cracking bag of roach they were, and the last rays of the sun turned them into bars of flame.

I have caught bigger fish, and bigger bags, but I have never made a more spectacular catch of fish than that. So what if the reservoir doesn't produce 2-pounders? I have a water, no great distance from my home, where I can go for a short evening session and expect to catch up to a dozen roach over a pound, with perhaps half of them over 1lb 8oz. What angler could ask for more?

You might look a bit surprised, too, if you had landed a 17lb 8oz pike, which took flavoured maggots in the dark!

THE HEAVY
FEEDER

Two miles from where I live I have the best river in England - the
Trent. It can be all things to all men - a dream for the dedicated
stick float man; a delight for the angler with a light spinning rod; an
arm-aching experience for the barbel man; and sheer despair for the
big carp fan who finds his 12lb line can make no impression on the
fish he has hooked. I have trodden all those paths, and many more,
with many triumphs and not a few defeats, but I have had my best
sport ever while feeder fishing this great river.

It may seem an odd confession from an author of such a book, but I
have voluntarily taken a year-long break from it. Endlessly taking huge
bags is almost as bad as endless blanks. I found myself not really trying
any more. The well of ideas had dried up because I couldn't think of
anything else I needed to know; there appeared to be nothing I could
learn. For me the quest for knowledge is the overriding motive for
fishing at all, and here was a subject I had totally cracked. It was a
unique experience for me, for I had always assumed that any kind of
fishing was a bottomless pit; a never-ending progression from one
problem to the next.

Here I had run out of problems, and the questions had evaporated. I
was reaping rich harvests for the time and thought previously invested,
but I woke up one morning and realised I was no longer enjoying it

half as much as I had done hitherto. Maybe a break will restore the old enthusiasm. I hope so, for I had some magical years on the feeder when it finally came together.

When I first started river feedering I used the block end, like almost everyone else, and I fished it sliding on the line. This served me well, with plenty of chub and an awful lot of barbel, which were my favourite species for a number of years. In fact barbel are the only species which have not responded vigorously to flavours, although this probably means that I have not found the right ones. I have caught a few on spicy baits, like curry, but to be honest, if you put a lot of hemp in the swim flavours seem almost superfluous for barbel. Maybe next year I will be hammering them out on Lobster Thermidor, or some other exotic concoction.

One thing I did learn about fast water fishing was that the sliding link can sometimes be better than the fixed paternoster, Once, on the Hampshire Avon, I was fishing my standard paternoster rig for barbel, with three grains of corn on a hook link of about two feet. I just could not get a bite, although I had seen fish in the swim. After about two hours I carefully peered into the gin clear water with polaroids, to see if there were any fish still there and to establish whether my bait was hidden in the weeds. My bait was there all right, wavering around about six inches off the bottom! I was sitting on a high bank, and the heavy flow had pulled my tackle taut. The end result looked like the illustration (Fig. 12). The problem was soon solved by lengthening

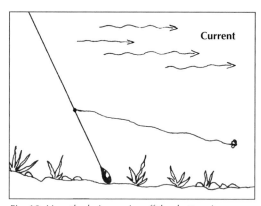

Fig. 12: How the bait can rise off the bottom in fast-flowing water

the hook link to 3ft, and putting a swanshot on the line about six inches from the hook. But it left me wondering how many hours I had sat fishing River Trent weir pools, trying to work out why the fish were not biting!

To successfully fish a strong flowing river like the Trent demands a heavy feeder, which in turn requires the right rod to cope with it. You

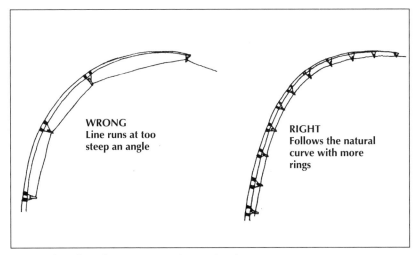

WRONG
Line runs at too
steep an angle

RIGHT
Follows the natural
curve with more
rings

Fig. 13: The right and wrong ways to ring a quivertip.

may well be casting four ounces or more, at times, and it is easy to break a rod with this loading. I have two rods for heavy feeder fishing, the Mal Storey Severn/Trent Carbon, which has two different tops, and the Terry Eustace Barbel Leger, in fibre glass. Both are quivertip rods, and both have the backbone to do the job. I would not be without either of them, yet I am not 100 per cent happy with these or any other commercial productions.

A feeder rod needs the rigidity of carbon to cope with the heavy casting, yet glass fibre is a far superior material for quivertips. So why not marry the two together? The quiver would need to be a long, slow taper affair, with at least twice as many rings as most commercial models are sold with. Without the extra rings an enormous amount of drag can be felt when winding in a heavy feeder, and the line actually makes a creaking noise. This doesn't happen on normal rods which are not fitted with quivertips, nor does it happen if you treat the quiver like a mini rod on its own, and ring it accordingly. Fig. 13 (above) shows the difference.

The first manufacturer who produces a fastish taper 10ft carbon rod, adds a two foot slow taper glass fibre quivertip to it, and lines it with rings which follow a natural and decreasing spacing right to the end of the tip, will have a potential market of 3m customers. Everyone will want one. Quivertips work at their best at right angles to the flow, yet so many anglers do insist on tilting the rod towards the feeder,

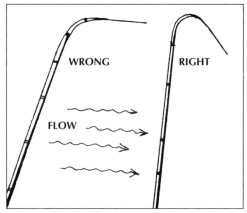

Fig. 14: Be sure to prop the rod at the correct angle.

destroying much of its sensitivity. The way to fish them properly is illustrated in Fig. 14. Before leaving the subject of quivers, a brief note for those who fish on into the dark, and want to fit a Betalight. Take off the tip ring and whip on a small single-legged Fuji ring about a quarter of an inch back from the end. Take half an inch of clear silicone rubber tubing, make a lateral hole in it with a needle and push it onto the quivertip so it points upwards, and Araldite it into position. When the glue has set push a Betalight about a quarter of an inch into the tubing, and that's it. It will not come out (see Fig. 15). Suction keeps it in place, and in nearly 20 years I have yet to lose a Betalight.

The reel is a matter of personal choice. Lots of them will do the job, just so long as there is no long casting to perform, and you might as well use 8lb line while you are at it. Heavy feeder fishing puts a terrific strain on the tackle, not to mention the wear and tear from scraping along the bottom and over snags.

It is when we come to the feeder itself that the real problems start. In

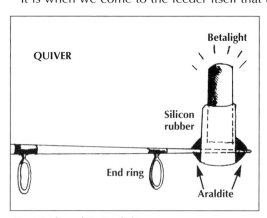

Fig. 15: The rod tip Betalight.

daylight hours the pressure from other anglers and boat traffic can keep the shoals well out in mid-river, but having beefed up the tackle in order to cope, reaching the fish is not a major problem. Sadly, what happens is the feeder starts to break up under the pounding it gets from being whacked to a distance

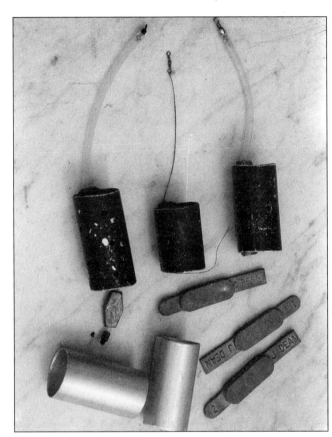

A selection of vacuum tube feeders, one unfinished, and some spare lead strips.

of 30 yards or so. This can spoil the fishing, especially if you haven't got another of the same weight, and find you can no longer hold in the right spot. I soon realised that I needed a light but very strong material, and I found it - aluminium vacuum cleaner extension tubes. When I realised how good they were I toured my local Currys and Comet shops, and others, and bought them all up. A serious local shortage of vacuum cleaner piping must obviously have developed, and I had visions of a legion of angry housewives!

At that time they were about £3.50 per tube, and I got seven big feeders out of each one, all about half as large again as the biggest Thamesly currently available. Making them was quite good fun. First I sawed them to length with a hacksaw, and drilled a few random holes. That meant I didn't have to tape any off. The next job was to sand and file all the rough edges smooth, and then I Araldited strips of lead onto

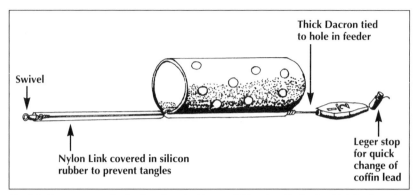

Fig. 16: The vacuum tube feeder, rigged with an additional coffin lead, which is slipped onto a length of Dacron tied to a hole in the end of the feeder. It is held in place with a leger stop. The coffin lead lies flat, like an extension of the feeder lead, and adds tremendously to the holding power in a strong flow.

them, of varying weights and thicknesses. I bought them from tackle shops, ranging in weight from 1.5 to 3.5oz, though I suppose strips of scrap sheet lead would do equally well. I drilled holes at the front to take thick nylon for the retaining cord, along with a swivel for easy attachment to the link. This I covered with silicone rubber to avoid tangles. I also drilled a hole in the trailing edge of the feeder and tied on a couple of inches of Dacron. This was to allow me to increase weight quickly by sliding on a coffin lead, plugging it in place with a leger stop. The last job was to give them a coat of matt green paint, and the Braddock/Hoover feeder was ready for action - totally indestructible in normal fishing conditions. (See photograph on the previous page, and Fig 16).

My approach to heavy feeder fishing is to lay down an extensive carpet of groundbait, laced with feed, so that when the shoals arrive they will usually stay there. The groundbait, with its appetising aromas, drifts downstream to attract the fish, and when they get there they find a carpet of hemp, wheat, groundbait or anything else I might chose to use. They start rooting around in it, and that activity brings in more fish.

I hope I know how it works by now. In my early days of pond and lake fishing I spent a lot of time up trees, observing fish and the way they behaved, and it was time well-spent. Hours at a time were expended, perched above the water, watching and learning. A small group of roach might start half-heartedly picking at the lake bed. Little puffs of silt would arise, interesting more roach. Then a cruising tench would take an interest, and get its head down as well. A large cloud would develop in the water, attracting still more fish. For an hour it would be frantic activity, until gradually an odd fish would drift away, then another, and finally it would all subside. Now if I could create that sort of activity, and sustain it, what sort of catches might be possible on a river like the Trent? I had a pretty good idea, but it worked beyond my wildest dreams - after a considerable amount of experimenting, of course. First the groundbait plugs had to be sorted out, and I finally settled on a base mix of two parts brown crumb and one part bran. With a quarter of a pint of water to each pint of dry mix it gives you just the sort of semi-dry texture needed to make it dissolve rapidly out of the feeder once it hits the bottom. I tried dozens of powder additives, mixed in with the crumb, and scores of flavours, which were added to the water used to dampen the crumb, plus various seeds for the filling.

The baits

Hemp was an obvious one, following my experience with barbel, and it also does well for bream, chub and roach, but I was never completely happy about it. I thought about the large number of anglers who were already using it, with float and feeder techniques, and worried that a large proportion of the fish may be associating it with danger, particularly the chub and carp, the two fastest learners in the fishy world.

Sweetcorn is very good, both as a hook-bait and as a feeder filler, and if the juice is added to the water used in the groundbait you have a really effective combination. There are drawbacks, though. Once again it has been used quite a lot, and it can be expensive in the amounts needed to make it work properly. It also seems to be very attractive to skimmers and hybrids, while not being particularly appealing to chub.

My next choice was wheat, which was and still is a superb bait and attractor. I will digress here, in the interests of economy. To get the best from seeds and particles often means using an awful lot, and even though many of them are quite cheap it soon mounts up. It pays, therefore, to find a seed warehouse and buy in bulk. I buy my wheat in 56lb bags, and sometimes I buy two at a time - 112lbs. Why not? It lasts for ages, without deteriorating. If you haven't a warehouse nearby ask for a deal at your local pet shop. You will find they can get all sorts of things when you are prepared to buy a sackful, rather than just asking for a couple of pounds.

Wheat, as with most seeds, absorbs water like a sponge, and it needs soaking for at least 24 hours before cooking. Cover it with two inches of excess water, as it swells up while absorbing moisture. Afterwards, simmer on a low light until the seeds just split. I don't weigh out my wheat. I do everything in pints, using a plastic measuring jug - seeds, maggots, groundbait, water, the lot. That way I always know I can repeat a successful combination next time. Used just as it is wheat is an excellent bait, but add a flavour and it becomes a truly outstanding fish attractor and bait, and not just in the summer and autumn, as tradition would have it. Because it is such an absorbent seed it takes a flavour very well, of course, and it is added at the soaking stage. The correct amount is 10ml. to the amount of water needed to cover three pints of wheat. I specify three pints, as that is a nice bucketful to take on a five or six hour session.

I doubt that you will manage to put that amount through a feeder, but you will probably need some in reserve, for use when the approach is becoming rather too successful. You will sometimes find that the swim really comes alive, and you have too many fish, all trying to occupy the same space - close to the feeder. You begin to suffer all sorts of knocks and pulls which you cannot connect with, and when this first happened to me I could not understand what was going on. I finally tried casting in without a bait on, and got just as many false bites. They were simply attacking the feeder itself and brushing into the terminal tackle. My approach was working too well, but I got over it. I split the fish up by catapulting loose wheat over a wider area, which still leaves the hook in the middle of the shoal. I went back to getting proper bites, and it is now a standard answer to that particular problem. Do not expect to drink much coffee while your bait is in the water.

I've spent a lot of time discussing wheat because it is just the size most anglers are happy with, and is both cheap and easily obtainable. You can take ten basic flavours - cheese, fish, spice etc. - and fish each one for just a season. At the same time you can add a colour (described later), and perhaps fish a blue Mango flavoured bait one year and a green Onion flavoured bait the next. At the end of 10 years you will find there are plenty of flavours and colours left to try. But tell me, when did you last see an angler using wheat? Even with the rocketting price of maggots the vast majority have not even tried to find a cheap substitute, and wheat is more than a substitute. It's better!

Maize is another real winner, but virtually unused by all but the carp anglers. It's really too hard for a hookbait, although I have used it successfully when the skimmers have been pestering me. It is a good feeder filler though, and a good fish attractor. It has the advantage of not needing boiling, but it must be soaked for at least 48 hours before use. It absorbs flavours very well, but if left to soak for more than two days it starts fermenting. In fact it smells something like a whisky distillery, and if left for five days it gets really evil. Take the lid off and it almost rears up and attacks you. I have used it, though, in all these stages, flavoured and unflavoured, fermenting and nearly toxic, and it works every time. Again I buy it by the hundredweight from the seed warehouse.

I have dabbled with plenty of other seeds - Chick Peas, Black-eyed Beans, Maples, Groats (flavoured or just fermented). It doesn't matter, for they all seem to work. If cost is no problem the new mini-boilies can be bought from tackle shops and used as both bait and as feeder fillers. Really it's endless, and I doubt that any angler will ever live long enough to try out all the combinations. But while he is trying he will have some great sport.

Going through some of my diaries, while preparing this book, I found an entry for Autumn, 1985, which was my second year of using seed baits. It says: "3 hours 45 minutes fishing, packed up at 9 p.m. Finished with 13 bream to 4lb 1oz, two others nearly 4lb, a chub of 3lb 1oz and a couple of 12oz roach. Not really on." Not on? I can remember days when a catch like that would have been the highlight of my season, but already I was getting to the stage where anything less than 50lb seemed like a failure.

The baits I used had a lot to do with the quality of the fish, as I always tried to give them something they would not be wary of. In my early days I used cheese a lot, following on with bread crust before deciding to use both of them together. Using a long-shanked hook I put a piece of crust on the bend and moulded a pyramid of cheese to it (see Fig. 17). It proved

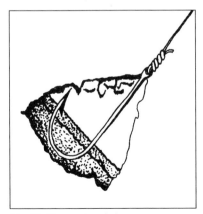

Fig. 17: The crust and cheese combination.

excellent. I had got to the stage where either bait on its own would produce odd fish, plucks or missed bites, but when the two were used together I got long, slow pulls on the quivertip which just kept on going until I struck. Bream, chub, roach, barbel and carp all loved it, and still do. In conjunction with cheese flavoured wheat in the feeder it is really deadly.

Another big one was my sausage special. Take a half pound of pork sausages out of their skins (for some reason this seems better than using skinless), and mix with crushed Weetabix until you have a firm paste. While kneading it I add in a tablespoon of Bovril, and boil Bovril into the seeds to be used in the feeder. To finish off I mix the groundbait plugs with diluted Bovril. Now that gives you a real meat flavoured attack, and it is a particularly good coloured water bait as well. One evening I was fishing the feeder and sausage meat in a swift 4ft deep run, and had taken a few nice chub, but I was hoping for a barbel. At last a firm bite found me attached to a fish which surged powerfully downstream, defying all my efforts on 7lb line for a good five minutes. Just when I was getting really excited my "barbel" broke surface - a pike weighing 9lb. Before the session ended I had also landed an eel of 2lb, and I have also had roach on sausage - unusual for them to take meat-based baits.

Yet another good bait is luncheon meat paste, which is made in the same way as the sausage bait, using Weetabix as a stiffener. With this bait I often used finely diced luncheon meat in the feeder, and alternate cubes of meat and paste on the hook. It is a real chub attractor but the bream love it too, as they do the sausage special. With both these baits I gear up the size of the bait and hook to the size of the fish I expect to catch - anything from pea size on a 14 hook to a pigeon's egg lump on a no. 4.

Around the same time I tried cockles and prawns, the cooked variety. Both are excellent baits for chub and barbel in rivers, and cockles are particularly effective for tench in stillwaters. Sheer cost makes it impractical to use them in the feeder, but there is a way round it. Among the scores of flavours available today are many which are fish and sea-food based, including Prawn Cocktail and Cockle. If you add a teaspoon of one of these flavours to a quarter pint of water, adding this to each dry pint of groundbait, you end up with a feeder filling which reeks of, say, cockle, but the only solid mouthful is on the hook. The bites, when they come, are truly vicious, threatening to take the rod off the rests and into the water. If I were to fish a match on a heavily-hammered river that held chub or barbel I would certainly try this approach.

Perhaps the most versatile bait I have used in conjunction with heavy feeder fishing, though, is a real golden oldie which is hardly ever used these days - bread paste. Flavouring bread paste goes back into the last century, probably, but the modern concentrated flavours have given this elderly offering a new lease of life. With ordinary white crumb in the feeder it will score particularly well with bream, plus the occasional carp, but flavour it and a whole new world opens up. It is very easy to do. Take an unsliced loaf, cut off the crusts and knead it into a paste, using about a quarter of a pint of water, adding more if necessary. To this water add 5ml (about a teaspoonful) of liquid flavouring.

Which flavour? I cover that in depth later on, but if there are any readers who do not know where to get them from just walk into a major tackle shop and you will see rows of small bottles - 50mls usually - lining the shelves. Just about any of them will work, some better than others for particular kinds of fish, some better on some waters than others. With these your simple paste can be made to smell like cheese, fish, garlic, curry or even cough mixture. Whichever one you choose, add the same to your groundbait or seeds, or both - but it does not need to be the same. How about cherry flavoured bait and tuna flavoured groundbait? Or strawberry or curry? There are hundreds of possible combinations. No, I haven't tried them all, and neither has anyone else, but I can give you a good guide as you read on.

During the time I have fished these pastes and specials I have gone out expecting to make big catches - expecting, not hoping - so effective did they become. I purchased a deep freeze (for my tackle room, not the kitchen) and froze up all my unused baits. This meant I could generally take out three different flavoured pastes, plus sausage or luncheon meat pastes, so ensuring that I would always have the right bait with me. I have even used them to good effect when they have spent a year in the back of the freezer.

I cannot emphasise too much how effective all these baits are, but I cannot remember the last time I saw anyone using them on the banks of the Trent, or anywhere else.

The hair rig

There comes a time, particularly on the really heavily-fished waters, when fish become shy of almost any method of bait presentation, and

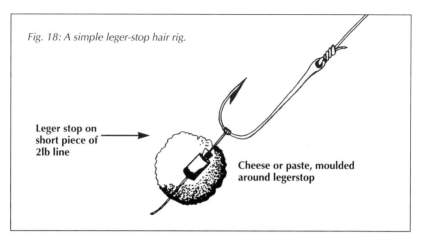

Fig. 18: A simple leger-stop hair rig.

Leger stop on short piece of 2lb line

Cheese or paste, moulded around legerstop

this is when what is commonly known as the hair rig can really bring a swim back to life. Most anglers think the hair rig is for carp fishing only, and far too technical for general use, but in fact it can be simplicity itself. The first time I tried it I was fishing the Derbyshire Dove, on the popular match water near Tutbury. The resident chub shoals were the target, and cheese was the bait. I was getting plenty of bites, but no fish. A series of little taps and trembles on the tip would subside, and I would wind in to find the bait missing. Now and again the tip would slam round in an unmissable bite - which I missed!

Clearly they were bait shy, and although I had never previously considered hair-rigging for anything other than carp it was clearly worth a try. The original idea of the hair was to fool carp which had become hook and bait shy, so why not the same solution for other species showing the same symptoms? I tied a length of 2lb line to the bend of the hook, and pegged on a leger stop - instant hair rig. I just moulded the cheese around the leger stop, and could have done the same with any of the baits mentioned in the previous section - bread, sausage, bread paste or whatever. As you will see from Fig. 18 it leaves the hook entirely bare, while the bait itself is apparently free of any encumbrance which might alarm the fish. When such a bait is sucked in the ironmongery follows it, of course, and you have yourself a fish.

How did it go on the Dove? Bingo! Every take became a strong, smooth pull, and I finished up with a good catch of chub and two barbel. The fish were probably still mouthing the bait as before, but could then find nothing to worry about - no metal on the first touch. They began to take with complete confidence.

There are smaller leger stops to suit smaller hooks and baits, and even small shot could be used to suit a tiny bait. The only point to watch is that there should be enough space between the bend of the hook and the bait to allow a cautious fish to mouth it without feeling metal. Providing that a short tag of line is left protruding beyond the leger stop it can be regularly adjusted while fishing, much as you adjust the bottom shot while trotting with a float.

I would fancy my chances of succeeding with this sort of presentation on the really hard waters, and the famous "road" stretch of the Trent at Burton Joyce comes to mind here. This is (or was before its decline in 1991/2) an area which helps to confirm my philosophy about baits and presentation. Matchmen tend to laugh at the idea that Trent fish are not inherently shy of strong line and big hooks, and they will say they sometimes can't get bites on 12oz lines and 22s. Not on straightforward maggot and caster, they can't, but what happened when wasp grub started to win the matches at Burton Joyce? Correct, they banned it, but weren't the grub men catching on big hooks and strong line. Yes, they were! Why? Because wasp grub is a super bait? Or merely a different bait, of which the fish are therefore less wary? If grubs were used at Burton Joyce with the frequency of maggots it would be a different story after a while.

My approach recognises that fish eventually become wary of baits, which is why I am constantly changing them, or making them smell like something different. The less bait wary they are the less they are tackle shy as well, but the mass approach to the Trent, and rivers like it, is almost purpose designed to make the fish difficult to catch. My first (and last) visit to Burton Joyce was a real culture shock. I was staggered to find anglers every 15 to 20 yards, on both banks, as far as they eye could see. I had deliberately chosen a mid-week day, and initially cursed my luck at dropping onto a big match. But it wasn't a match. It was simply that several hundred anglers had the same idea as me - a few hours' fishing. Doesn't anybody go to work any more? I became aware of the constant plop-plop-plop - one every second - and it continued all day. It was the sound of block-end feeders endlessly hitting the water. Not one angler that I saw was using an open-ended feeder, though I do know they are used more often since the area began to produce big bream weights. I tried to work out how many pints of maggots went into that stretch of river daily, but it was impossible to calculate. Obviously such areas must sustain a head of fish far in excess of those nature herself could support.

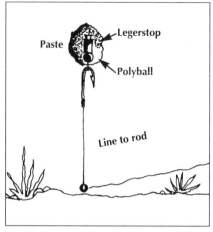

Fig. 19: Pop-up paste, fished on a polyball hair rig.

With everyone fishing the same way angling is reduced to a lucky dip, but the man with a hair rig, and perhaps something a bit different in the way of bait, is the likeliest to score. Indeed, that thought triggers the memory again. It isn't only wasp grub which makes my case. In the past two seasons raw steak, fished on far stronger tackle than maggots, has been so successful at Burton Joyce they are now talking of banning that as well! If you do start winning on sausage, paste or whatever it may be wise not to talk about it!

But let me return to the hair rig. There is a possible further modification with the leger stop, which is quite easily done. Buy a bag of those small polyballs which many tackle shops now sell, often in mixed sizes. Make a hole in one and thread it on the hair line between hook and stop. The bait is then shaped around both the polyball and the stop, which helps to counteract the weight of the hook, and also prevents the bait sinking into soft weed or mud. By reducing the paste a little bit at a time you can arrive at a very slow sinking bait, which will lift and flutter attractively when fish are active near it. You can also make the bait so buoyant it needs a small shot to hold it down. It will suspend an inch or so off bottom like a tethered balloon (see Fig. 19). This sort of set-up has been developed to catch heavily pressured carp,

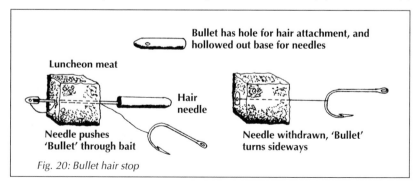

Fig. 20: Bullet hair stop

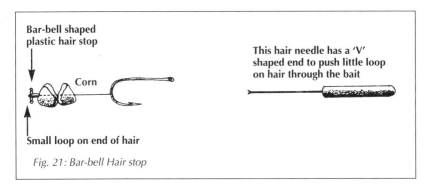

Bar-bell shaped plastic hair stop

Corn

This hair needle has a 'V' shaped end to push little loop on hair through the bait

Small loop on end of hair

Fig. 21: *Bar-bell Hair stop*

but I doubt if there is a carp in the country which is more pressured than the fish at Burton Joyce!

It is obvious that the leger stop hair rigs are suitable only for the mouldable baits like pastes. To use luncheon meat and several other baits on a hair demands the use of different hair stops, and the passing of the hair through the baits with a baiting needle. You can either steal a needle from the wife's sewing box, or buy a purpose-designed job from a tackle shop. Two of the best methods are illustrated in Figs 20 and 21. In Fig. 20 a small plastic bullet, tied to the hair, is pushed through the bait. When the needle is withdrawn the bullet turns sideways and acts as a stop for such baits as luncheon meat, prawns, cockles, stewing steak and fish chunks. In Fig 21 a hair rig with a loop is passed through such baits as sweetcorn, wheat, maize and so on, and stopped with a barbel-shaped plastic hair stop which, like the little bullet, is available from specialist shops. Both types are a little fiddly to tie on the bank, so I tie mine to a variety of hook lengths at home, storing them on pole winders. On the bank I can bait up in seconds.

The bolt rig

We all experience those days when we know the river is going to be tough going. It is either up and dirty, or extremely cold - maybe a mixture of both. It may be lashing with rain or blowing a gale. Float fishing is going to be a waste of time, and a delicate quivertip approach nearly as bad. Nothing much is going to feed anyway and, on top of that you are maybe fishing a match, and have drawn a duff peg. Faced with this situation most anglers will stick on a lobworm and hope for the odd chub. That's all that may be feeding, but it is essential not to miss the few bites which may come your way. That's where the bolt rig comes in. First you increase the lead on the feeder to way above the amount needed to hold bottom. In fact you are trying to nail it to the bottom, and the feeder link is shortened to about three inches.

It is questionable who first invented the bolt rig, but we got the name from the carp anglers. Some matchmen were using it prior to that, while calling it something else. I can remember Colin Dyson writing about winning matches in flood conditions simply by allowing fish to hook themselves against the weight of a heavy bomb. He developed it for gudgeon, and was surprised to find that he also hooked big roach and various other species. He wouldn't claim to be the first with the idea either; it probably goes back into the last century (which he doesn't, quite!). What matters, though, is that carp and other fish will pick up a bait and bolt as a first reaction when they bump into a heavy weight, be it a bomb or a feeder. If they felt slight resistance they might spit the bait out instead, but the panic induced by a sudden, hard jolt just makes them run, with the bait still in their mouths. They either hook themselves or are hooked when the angler reacts to the bite; either way the fish is usually yours.

My bolt rig method for difficult conditions is the over-heavy feeder, but I don't use lobworm, because everyone else is doing that. I go for baits which I have found to be deadly at such times, but retain the flavours in the groundbait, which must match the bait in use. I go for meat or fish in these scratching situations. If it is meat it's either sausage or a cube of luncheon meat, and in either case I use them big! My sausage paste will be a ball an inch or more in diameter, and the luncheon meat an inch-plus square, sometimes even bigger than that. Fellow anglers who see me casting such baits have themselves a good laugh, and take the mickey - until I start catching, that is. I have no idea why such baits are preferred in such conditions; I only know that they are. I have sat there with normal-sized offerings and attracted either the occasional tap or nothing at all. Put a monster bait on and wallop! Over goes the rod. There is no warning, it's just a full-blooded take.

One can theorise about it. Maybe the groundbait has attracted the fish upstream, but it can't easily find a small bait in the murk. The great lump is easier to see, and it is of a size which causes no alarm in a wary fish. It doesn't associate the lump with danger, because it has never seen a bait that size before. Once again, it's different...

Most of the time the fish which fall to this approach are big - chub and barbel upwards of 2lb, plus an odd carp, but do not be surprised to catch a fish as small as 1lb. Somehow they manage to cram these huge baits into their mouths, though even a 1lb chub has a cavernous mouth. If the area is noted for chub, though, I will fish with chunks of fish, but don't expect any bonus carp or barbel. Fish is a deadly bait, particularly for the bigger chub, and has in fact caught me more chub over 4lb than any other bait. It is not exactly an open secret, even in the specialist field, but a while back a series of headline-making chub were reported from a lake in my area. It was never admitted, but they all fell to strips of mackerel and pieces of smelt.

River fish have the same tendency, and I have proved it to my own satisfaction on many occasions on the Trent where, you may or may not have noticed, there are two types of chub. One is long and slimly proportioned, even when large, and turns up on all sorts of baits like maggot, caster, bread, cheese etc. The other sort are short, and incredibly deep for their length, and shaped like common carp. They become extremely predatory very early in life, and quite often take spinners or livebaits intended for perch or pike. Other than that they become mainly nocturnal, laying up under cover all day and coming out at night to scavenge. They seem vulnerable in the day time only or mainly in the conditions we are discussing here. In thick, murky water they lose a lot of their natural caution, and will take a bait with confidence, providing they have not learned to be wary of it. Such a bait is a chunk of dead sea fish.

I have tried them all, natural deadbaits and sea fish, and although gudgeon can be good, as can sprat, I'll settle for a chunk of mackerel or sardine. The heavy oiliness of both these fish is a great attraction, and for the specimen hunters among you these are the baits, believe me. In a known chub swim, in normal conditions, sprat chunks can be deadly too. Fish a chunk

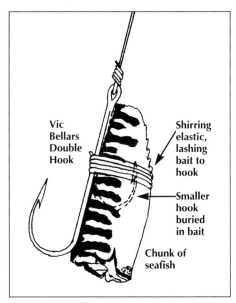

Vic Bellars Double Hook

Shirring elastic, lashing bait to hook

Smaller hook buried in bait

Chunk of seafish

Fig. 22: The fish chunk rig for chub.

on a big hook, or hair rig, and fill the feeder with mashed sprat.

As with meat, I use the fish in big pieces, but I have to admit having a spell where I had a lot of missed bites. This can be solved to some extent by using a hair rig in conjunction with a large hook. Unfortunately for matchmen the best rig I have developed cannot be used by them, thanks to the two hook rule, though it is arguable whether the Vic Bellars double counts as two hooks, or one with two branches! Anyway, the rig I use is illustrated in Fig. 22 (previous page). It was developed for pike fishing with small deadbaits and half herrings and mackerel, and is amazingly effective for that purpose, but I found it the same for chub when I adapted it.

For those who might like to try it, the smaller branch of the size 6 double is buried in the bait, and the larger hook is lashed at 90 degrees to the bait with shirring cotton - elasticated thread obtainable from any needlecraft shop. I take the baits to the water frozen, which makes this job easier. As the bait thaws in the water the cotton contracts, keeping that large hook locked upright. The fish can neither take the bait off the hook - which they are very good at if they get the chance - nor can they pick up the bait and avoid the hook. They have to grab it properly, bolting when they feel the weight of the feeder or the hook, or both!

There are some monstrous chub in the Trent. My best at the time of writing is a little over 6lb, but I know of several bigger than that. I am expecting the river to produce a genuine seven-pounder at any time, and see no reason why the Trent should not eventually produce a new national record - to me, I hope!

FLAVOURS
and
ADDITIVES

I had wondered whether to put this chapter at the end, but maybe it is time to take a little break from the the "how and what to do" stuff, even though some of my most important discoveries and techniques have still to be covered. It is perhaps the logical place to cover flavours and additives anyway, for I was developing my overall approach and my knowledge of this key subject at the same time. Just as it all came together on the flavour/additive side I was to learn a method of fishing with the feeder which was the final piece of the jigsaw. The combined effect on my results was devastating, to say the least.

I suspect a lot of you actually bought the book for this bit, so I won't keep you waiting any longer. I will attempt to introduce you, in as simple and straightforward a way as I can, to what the top carp anglers have discovered about additives and flavours, and how this knowledge can be used in the pursuit of other fish. I was a carp man, myself, way back in the sixties, and I am currently engaged in one particular branch of that game where there is still a lot to learn - river carping. From 1960 to 1970 I was a dyed-in-the-wool carp fanatic. Nothing else mattered during the summers and autumns of those years, and even in the winter I would have a go if the lakes were not frozen over. My baits were bread, crust, worms, potatoes and mussels. Even sweetcorn and luncheon meat were still in the future. I night-fished every weekend, and generally spent as much time as I could on the water. All that

*The writer with a 14lb
12oz carp from the River
Trent, where he has
proved beyond doubt that
carp bait 'technology' is
applicable to other
species of fish.*

effort gave me less than a dozen doubles in a season, plus a few
smaller fish, and my total of 20-pounders was only five over the
decade. That would not impress the carp angler of today, but my
results were excellent for that period, when good carp waters were few
and far between. Nowadays there are several anglers who catch
hundreds of doubles in a season, with many 20-pounders, even several
thirties or a forty.

Tackle and rigs have improved out of sight, a little of which I have
described, but apart from the actual growth in the number and quality
of carp waters the biggest single breakthrough has been the use of
flavours. By the time these came on the scene I had moved on to
barbel fishing, but found I could not ignore what was happening on
the carp scene. What really interested me were the constant reports of
"nuisance fish" - species other than carp which showed too much of a
liking for particular baits and flavours. So successful were some of
these baits in the attraction of unwanted species that many had to be
abandoned. Several times carp fanatics told me that "the roach just
wouldn't leave it alone," or "the tench went barmy on it" when
describing a flavour they had given up on, and they were quite happy

to tell me what it was.

I have been collecting this sort of information for years and now, after hundreds of sessions using flavours for nearly everything that swims, I will stick my neck out and make a few statements that many may find hard to believe. There is a flavour which will turn on the particular specie you want to catch. I will go further. I believe there is a flavour to catch the smaller fish of each species, and a different flavour to catch the larger fish of each species. If you have accepted that, I will now tell you what the flavours are, and you can go out yourself and just wind them in. Yes? Sorry, it's not quite as simple as that, I am afraid.

All waters are different, and what turns roach on in a river can be a positive turn-off on the nearby lake, or on a totally different river. The smell which murders bream in July will not produce a bite in February. So, what you have to do is sort out what will do the business on your waters throughout the season. Those who fish the Trent are really in luck, though, for everything which works for me will work for them. I would be surprised if the rest of you cannot swiftly sort out your own waters, using the information and guidelines which follow.

There *are* some rules which apply in all cases. I have found that the softer flavours, sweet, fruity and creamy, for example, are very good in summer, but hit and miss in the autumn and winter. As the water gets colder the spicy, hotter flavours will work best, which means you must carry a thermometer and check the water temperature regularly. I can hear some of you saying: "I don't need one of those. What's the point? I can't alter the water temperature, whatever it is..."

Agreed, but what you can do is note the temperature on each visit, and record what works and what doesn't at each temperature level, until you get it right every time out. That means keeping a diary, of course, but it will become invaluable as you go along. I have written this whole book from my diaries, and it wasn't until I started going back through them for several years that I realised just how much invaluable information I really had tucked away in there. Yes, I have learned from my own book! Just one example: Until I put together the section on perch, which follows, I had not realised just how often curry flavour turns on these fish. I had missed that, and quite a lot more. You cannot fully trust your memory, however good you think it is.

Diaries, thermometers, depthometers... it all seems like a lot of trouble, doesn't it? Well, I can't give you a magic bait which will always catch, but I can give you some magical fishing if you are prepared to go for it. It is all about using the right flavour at the right time, and perhaps the easiest way to start to get it across is to describe a few of my fishing trips - the fish I caught and what I used to catch them with.

The first flavour I ever used was cheese, mixed into a simple bread paste as described earlier, at a level of 5ml to a crustless loaf. I settled for 5ml purely because this was the level recommended on the bottle for 1lb of carp bait. I have learned that you can go higher or lower, and experience suggests that chub and bream will accept higher levels, while carp and roach are more sensitive, and respond to less than 5ml. Try it yourself, and see. Nowadays there are several cheese flavours to be had, Blue Cheese, High Cheese, Gorgonzola and others. I have not tried them all, but have no doubt they will work. Where you see the letters E.A. after the name - i.e. High Cheese E.A. - it means the flavour is based on a rapidly evaporating ethyl alcohol. This makes it disperse into the water at a far faster rate than normal, which is ideal for the matchmen. It is also dearer, but not necessarily better. Again, you will have to try it and see.

For my first cheese session on the Trent, where most of my river fishing is done, I used hemp in the feeder plus some cheese flavour in the groundbait. I also took along several other baits, as I had no way of knowing then if the cheese paste was going to work. Early in the session I used ordinary cheese, crust, flake and my sausage special. It was a lovely warm evening in late August, and the water was low and running at 72 deg. F. due to the power station influence - a constant factor on the Trent.

Cheese produced the usual plucks and pulls from the skimmers and the odd sharper jab on the quiver, none of which could be struck. Flake gave me nothing, which was not unexpected in the clear water, but the sausage produced my first fish, a bream of about 2lb. A couple more, slightlly smaller, soon followed. The cheese/crust combination I described earlier produced two chub of 2lb 8oz and 3lb 1oz, so things were definitely looking up. I was using the big vacuum tube feeders, so every cast was putting down a good helping of food. After about an hour I moulded a thumbnail-sized piece of paste around my size 8 hook, and made my first cast ever with a flavoured bait. All was still for about two minutes, before the tip bounced once and went smoothly round in an ever-increasing curve. The strike met more resistance than it had thus far in the session, and I soon netted a fine bream of 4lb 3oz. Nobody can say bream really fight, but hit a Trent fish 20 yards

Trent chub don't come much better than this - 6lb 1oz, and it fell to a flavoured bait.

downstream, in 12ft of moving water, and it is like hitting a brick wall. They have to be pumped back upstream, all the while giving solid thuds on the rod, which is why a lot come off when you use small hooks. The next cast brought another just short of 4lb, and then two more just over.

The bites started to come within seconds of the feeder hitting bottom, and some of them I missed. I put these down to smaller fish, as I was now getting all sizes from 4lb 8oz down to barely 1lb. I only took one more chub, a small one, during that first session, which I finished after just over 4 hours 30 minutes with nearly 60lb of fish in the net. Not a bad start on flavoured baits!

My mind was buzzing with all this throughout the next day in the office, and I just had to go back that evening. Results were just as good - another large bag, and although the paste was catching the majority of the fish, most of them bream, the sausage and cheese/crust also caught, and produced the only chub bites that I had. A couple of days later, on my third trip (yes, it is nice to live so close to the river!) there was a slight level and flow increase, due to recent rain, and a water temperature drop to 66 degrees F. This slowed things a little, and the sausage and cheese/crust shared equal honours with the paste. I included two roach of nearly 1lb each in the catch, to sausage, which totalled only 40lb (shame!).

This gave me my first clue that different flavours may be needed in different conditions; something I did not realise at the time. I picked it up when going though my diary at the end of the season. Yes, that diary again. Apart from the catches and the baits used I record the water temperature, the level and the weather. I think it was Dick Walker who said "Most anglers don't know where they are going, don't know where they are when they get there, and don't know where they have been when they get back."

Thanks to my records I know everything I have done over the last 20 years, and I re-live my whole season's fishing at the time I miss it most - in the close season. The diaries are a treasure, and if you need any further motivation remember what Mae West once said: "Keep a diary... one day it will keep you!"

Next time out the level was back down again, the water was up to 71 degrees F. and I tried out something different. I swapped the hemp for wheat and added cheese flavour to it during the cooking. As I walked down to the river with a bucket of 'cheese' wheat in one hand, cheese smelling groundbait in the other, plus paste in my back pack, I must have absolutely reeked. The wife says I always do, but I ignore such cutting remarks.

The bream came again, and in numbers and quality, with the paste way ahead of the other baits. This time I caught two good chub on it as well, by using it in combination with the crust, instead of real cheese and crust. I even had a couple of nice roach on it. This impressed me so much I kept swapping between real cheese and the cheese flavoured paste, and proved beyond doubt that the artificial was taken *in preference* to to the real thing, in conjunction with the crust.

There was something else I learned in that session. During one cast the paste flew off, but I left it, thankful of the chance to have a coffee. Then I watched in amazement as the tip continued to twitch and jerk for nearly a minute. The fish were attacking the feeder! With a feeling almost of awe I began to feel I was really onto something. Over the following seasons this feeder attack was to become a commonplace occurrence. Is there more positive proof that the fish wanted what I was offering?

I made my next cast with the mind whirling again, and settled back to try and work out the implications of what I had just experienced. The next thing I knew the rod butt was hitting me hard as it literally leaped out of the rests. Carp! I never stood a chance. It went downstream like a train, and when I tried to slow it down it cracked off my 4.5lb hook link with complete contempt. With shaking hands I tied up a 6lb link, finding that it did not slow the bream down at all. Half an hour later I hooked another downstream express, but it didn't feel as big as the other. Five minutes later I landed a beautiful common carp of 8lb 8oz.

I did not continue. First my mind was in a daze with it all, and I found I could not get to sleep that night. Secondly I had by now attracted a crowd of anglers around me. As I had been out-fishing everyone on the river they naturally wanted to know what the bait was. "Cheese," I said innocently, knowing that my peg reeked of the fumes. I don't like to deceive people, but I had done the groundwork and did not want to give it all away just yet. As it was I did not get into that swim again for the rest of the season.

Not that it mattered, for wherever I took my 'special' I heaved out the bream, plus chub and roach, and the occasional carp. In fact they started to turn up regularly, every other trip, and I was now landing a lot more of them because I had stopped using anything less than 6lb line. I did not land them all, by any means. Some fish were hooked which totally ignored the tackle, breaking away with ease. What can you do with fish which simply roar off downstream without even slowing down, never mind stopping? It just leaves you totally inadequate. I didn't know it then, but they were to do exactly the same to me, on 12lb line, in later years.

As autumn turned into winter, and the water cooled, results slowed down. I began to try all sorts of extra baits, like redworms, lobworms, luncheon meat and so on, and they began to produce different fish - more chub, and even the odd barbel. Clearly the cheese paste was a warm water, summer level bait. Still, I ended the season with a huge record of catches - 50lb, 75lb, even 100lb, including carp to 15lb, chub to 4lb, roach to 1lb 8oz and masses of bream to 5lb 1oz. I could not wait for the following season.

The close season sped by in feverish activity. I located my nearest seed warehouse and bought sacks of wheat, maize, groats etc. I looked through the specialist catalogues and ordered flavours by the dozen. I even bought my own fridge, and a freezer to store all the special pastes I was busily making up. (Cost me a new lounge carpet that did. Funny how all women say "... if you've got the money for that then I want..."). But who cared? That new season was looming up, and it was almost like being sixteen again.

During my close season shopping spree I was in a tackle shop on Saturday afternoon, purchasing a bottle of Biotrak, which had just been put on the market. With my expanding knowledge of flavours the claims made for this product seemed excessive, but I had to give it a try. An angler noticed what I had bought and said, loudly and disparagingly: "That stuff will never do you any good; it's knowing where to find the fish that's important. Don't waste your money." I didn't argue, for that sort of blinkered ignorance can never be educated. What our friend did not realise is that flavours will trigger a feeding response from fish when ordinary baits fail. I firmly believe that, carried by the currents, the right flavour will draw fish into a swim they may not normally inhabit - very handy, when the chap in the next peg is sitting on a shedful.

This time I let a couple of mates in on the secret, not entirely out of friendship either! There were so many flavours to try I realised I could never do all the field testing myself. It would be more than useful to be trying more than one new bait at the same time, and to keep a close eye on the results. I did not think it could possibly get better, but it did. All three of us were hammering fish from the word go.

One of the lads kicked off with a 20lb mirror carp on sweetcorn paste - not the juice from the tin, but a flavour from one of the little bottles. As most of these are chemically produced they probably taste very different to the fish, but what matters is they work. Luncheon meat essence was another good one. Again it smelled nothing like the real thing, but it caught the fish. Hemp flavour wasn't remotely like hemp, but it produced another carp of 17lb for the angler who landed the 20-pounder. He was becoming quite impressed with the new technology! Hemp also proved to be one of the flavours which worked both in summer and winter.

Many of the flavours I use are marketed by Catchum, but other companies market equally good attractors, some of which are duplicated. You will find that every firm has Strawberry, Strawberry Cream and Strawberry something or other, for this has been one of the most effective flavours for the carp men since the boiled bait method began. The same goes for Chocolate Malt, Scopex and Maple Cream, and they all work for species other than carp. Rod Hutchinson originated them, and they were so successful others rushed to copy them.

All these flavours worked for me, and my friends, but the difficulty was to find something which did not work, at some time or another.

A nice brace of perch, weighing 2lb 4oz and 2lb 8oz. This species, too, falls for the right flavour, as you will read later in this chapter.

Hemp is particularly good, for apart from those bonus carp it proved remarkably effective for other species. It even produces a lot of chub, which most of the sweet pastes do not do. That may change, of course, as further favours are tried. Up to now I have tested about 50, but there are another couple of hundred to get through, plus others which come on the market every year. During that second season we tried all sorts of experiments, and they were getting more and more bizarre. How about cheese-flavoured lobworms? Curry flavoured sweetcorn? Pineapple flavoured luncheon meat? Again they all worked, and our combined catches for that summer were phenomenal. We caught carp, many of them big doubles, chub, which were mostly over 3lb, lots of roach over 1lb and endless bags of bream, with scores between 4lb and 5lb. It just went on and on.

It was almost impossible to further speed up the catch rate, so now I set about trying to improve the quality of the bait and groundbait in an attempt to catch an even better class of fish. Once again I buried my head in the mass of carp fishing literature, for there is no doubt that this branch of angling has advanced far ahead of the rest, certainly in the bait department.

Today's carp anglers would laugh at bread in any form, but I would never agree with them. I have seen too many big Trent carp taken on flake and the flavoured pastes - fish up to 32lb - to ever discard bread entirely. I had made it work with the help of carp fishing technology, but there was more than liquid flavourings to try. The carp men use powdered additives as well, and I figured it was time to give them a try.

Walk into any large tackle shop and, below the flavour bottles, you will see loads of plastic bags with labels on. When you read up on the properties of these powders some of the claims made about them seem almost ludicrous, but of course you are now in the realms of the big carp world, where everything is hyped up to make the angler believe that without this latest concoction he cannot possibly catch fish. I fell into the same trap and bought just about everything at first, but gradually whittled it down to a manageable level. Do not bother with things like Lactalbumin, Calcium Caseinate and Casein 30 Mesh, for these are basically for the high protein fanatic, who pays a great deal of money for these expensive products. There are many others which work very well, so I will list the powdered additives I have used, and how I rate them.

CODLIVINE: *This is a coarse, dark red powder produced as a mineral supplement for cattle feed. It is made from fish offal, smells very strongly, and will turn both paste and groundbait a brownish red. I add 1oz to my ball of paste, and 4oz to three pints of groundbait mix. It can be used in conjunction with any one of the liquid flavours. I have found it to be excellent. The carp books all suggest how good (or in their case bad) it is for tench, but I have found it to be a winner for Trent chub. My seed warehouse supplied it, and I got a 3lb 8oz bag for the same price which 12oz costs in tackle shops!*

SHRIMP MEAL, MACKEREL MEAL, CAPELIN, TROUT FRY CRUMB: *All can be used at the same level as Codlivine. The last two tend to clog the groundbait mix, but you can avoid that problem by using only 2oz to three pints of groundbait. All smell strongly, and can be made to stink mightily with the addition of a liquid flavour like lugworm. The wife may leave you, and no other angler will fish within 50 yards, but you will bag up with chub. I once made up a bait using all these fish meals together, and added some soya flour and seafood flavoured water until I had a firm paste. It was another surefire chub bait, which also attracted a high proportion of eels. Not bootlaces, mind you, but the bigger "snakes" in the 2 to 3lb class.*

MEAT AND BONE MEAL, BEEF AND HIDE MEAL, FEATHER MEAL:
Again use as for Codlivine, and these meals will give you a meaty approach. Use with meat-based flavours, of which Catchum's Savoury Meat is a very good example. It attracts chub and barbel, but the bream find it quite acceptable, as do the carp.

LIVER POWDER: *Expensive, but a very good additive to meat-based pastes, or even just plain bread paste. One ounce is enough, and do not add it to the groundbait. It is too expensive for that, and it clogs the groundbait anyway. I tried ordinary Bovril with this instead of a flavour, two teaspoons in the paste and a desert spoonful in the groundbait. Everything took it, especially the chub, and I even had a 1lb perch on it.*

LACTOPRO: *A smooth, creamy milk powder which improves the taste and the feel of bread paste (to me, anyway). Using 1oz to each pint of groundbait mix helps to give it a cloudy effect in the water, and it is ideal for use with all the creamy, fruity and sweet flavours. I rate it highly.*

SOYA FLOUR: *A cheaper powder which helps to bind your paste together and smooth it out. It also gives it a slightly different taste. I use it if I accidentally make my paste too wet. Do not add it to groundbait, for it clogs. There is a product available from the burgeoning health shops called Soyolk, based on soya and much cheaper. At 1991 prices it was 58p for 375 grammes (15oz). It is soya based and contains 40% protein, plus fibre, making it an ideal additive for any paste. For the carp men among you it's a first class boilie ingredient, and can be used as 50 per cent of your base mix.*

SEMOLINA: *A very useful ingredient when you do not have a loaf handy. Using 75% semolina and 25% Lactopro you can make a good alternative to bread paste. It is smooth and creamy, and dissolves slowly, thereby releasing any added flavour slightly faster. It is ideal for use with any of the fast "leak-off" Ethyl Alcohol (E.A.) flavours. I am still experimenting with this type of paste for winter, when ordinary bread paste loses much of its effectiveness.*

COLOURS: *Among the shelves of additives you will find plastic tubs of colour powders, used for producing boilies in different shades.*

They work just as well for pastes, simply by adding a teaspoonful at the mixing stage. They also work with groundbait at the rate of one heaped teaspoonful to three pints of dry mix. How do you fancy having a black ball of paste with a feeder full of pink groundbait? No problem, just give any colour you fancy a try. Should groundbait be neutral coloured, so as not to alarm the fish, or should it be brightly coloured to attract them? I feel there is a lot of room for experiment here.

VITMIN, VITREX, KELP: *All these powders are rich in vitamins and minerals, and carp anglers add them to boilies just to boost the quality of the bait. One side-effect is that it improves the general health of the fish, and is a way of giving something back to the sport. It is worth using for that reason alone, but there is a school of thought that suggests fish can recognise these essential substances, and will seek them out. That's a chance I cannot afford to miss, so I add them at half an ounce to the paste and 1oz to three pints of groundbait.*

SPICES AND HERBS: *A friend I took fishing with me remarked on the mouth-watering aroma given off by my groundbait bucket. I was on curry at the time, and it reminded him of the special dishes he was always having at home. My ears pricked up, and under intensive questioning - more like third degree, actually - he revealed that he had discovered a mini supermarket in Derby, run by Asians. One Saturday afternoon I made my way there, and uncovered a veritable Aladdin's Cave of possible bait additives. There were rows of 1lb packets of things like paprika, curry, cummin, chilli and many more. The garlic powder was an extremely fine flour, and particularly potent. One teaspoonful of this would have a pound of paste practically walking on its own, and would heavily flavour three pints of groundbait. There were also the Masalas, ready-mixed bags of spices which find their way into hot Indian meals. Garam, Tandoori and Fish Masalas were three I tried to good effect, just by adding them to the groundbait at 1oz per pint. On top of this there were also good-sized bags of things like chick peas, black-eyed beans and other seed baits, at knock-down prices compared to the specialist bait suppliers or main supermarkets. I now have an annual trip to this shop, which gives me plenty of ideas for each new season.*

GROATS: *I briefly mentioned these seeds earlier, and although I have not used them a lot as yet I do feel they are worth much more attention.*

They are a small, white seed, a bit like miniature wheat, and they only need soaking, not cooking. Left for four days, covered with water, they really ferment, giving off a milky liquid that has a very strong and unusual smell. No flavour is needed, and when I use them I mix the liquid with my groundbait, not seeing the need for any other additive. I have caught fish each time I have used groats, either with maggot or various pastes as the hook bait. I have noticed that I seem to catch more roach on these occasions. The milky liquid could be used to flavour bread paste, or maybe even maggots, and small hook advocates may even try to use them on the hook. They are certainly an attractor for carp, and can be obtained from seed warehouses or specialist bait suppliers.

I imagine that by now you are scratching your heads and wondering where to start, but do not forget that I had wonderful results with just bread paste and a liquid flavour. That simple approach will work for many years to come, but if you really cannot be bothered with any of that there is a method which, on its day, can be as effective as any of the highly charged "specials." Put simply, it is redworms and compost. A redworm or brandling on the hook, with the rotted down gunge they inhabit in the feeder, has given me some excellent bags of fish in rivers and stillwaters. I have a large container in my back garden in which I dump all my lawn cuttings, plus any waste vegetable matter I can get hold of. Once a year I load it with fallen apples from my trees, which gives a real booster to the worm population. If you don't have apples it is worth buying a few pounds, so good is the effect. When it all rots down you are left with a rich brown mixture which some fools use on their garden plants. What a waste! The mixture is heaving with redworms and brandlings, and a bucketful will give you all you need for bait and feeder filling for a day's fishing. My own wormery has been going strong for 15 years.

Flavoured maggots

The large catches I had made with all the pastes and seeds had boosted my confidence so sky high that I felt I could catch a mahseer from the Grand Union Canal if I tried - but only in the summer. No matter what I used the results started to slow once the water temperature fell below 60 degrees F., in rivers and in stillwaters. It was time to look for something else - flavouring maggots - and once again it was to make some huge catches.

It started gently enough. I had read a magazine article about a couple of lads who had been feeder fishing a gravel pit, and fishing side by side they had experienced far more bites on flavoured maggots than plain ones. Mainly small fish had been taken, but as they had been fishing the usual block end feeder on a very busy water it looked a promising avenue to explore. Their flavour was called Red Zing, marketed by Geoff Kemp baits, and although it was quite expensive, and sold in large bottles only, I sent for some. Talk about hot! The tiniest spot on the tongue would leave it stinging for at least 15

The author with a 4lb 11oz chub from the Derbyshire Derwent

minutes, and just sniffing the bottle was enough to make the eyes water.

I deliberately did not tell my companion what I was doing first time out, on the Trent, because I needed a genuine comparison with plain maggots. In the event I caught twice as many fish as he did, mainly small roach, skimmers, perch and gudgeon. It was autumn, and I had not then made the connection between "hot" flavours and cold water, but this seemed a good start.

The weather had changed for my next trip, about a week later, with a cold wind and the water down to 57 degrees F. Nevertheless, things started looking up. With Zing on the maggots, at 5ml. to the pint, and sweetcorn flavour in the groundbait, the fish came regularly. I finished up with a dozen net roach to 1lb 3oz, four chub to 3lb 4oz, ten perch to 1lb 12oz and a load of skimmers and gudgeon. I was particularly impressed with the roach, which are not at all easy to catch on the feeder in the Trent, or anywhere else, for that matter.

The bites had been fast, as they usually are, but they kept the tip going round long enough for me to hit them, which wasn't usual. All these fish were taken on a 3.6lb Ultima hook length to a size 14 eyed round bend hook, baited with 2 to 3 maggots. Most Trent feeder men would cringe at this tackle, but I have never fished finer than this on the river unless I have used float tackle.

It was winter for my next trip, December, and the water was down to 50 degrees F. This time I let my pal in on the secret, even flavouring his maggots for him. He promptly got his own back on me by taking a super net of roach, a dozen of which were 1lb to 1lb 14oz, plus one absolute beauty weighing 1lb 15oz. He had also spiced his groundbait with 3oz of Tandoori Masala, which seemed a perfect complement to the Zing. And so began the best winter's feeder fishing I had ever had.

I concentrated on the roach at first, fishing swims and areas I knew held quality fish. Keeping the Red Zing as the bait flavour I alternated Zing, Hemp, Curry and Rod Hutchinson's Ultraspice in the groundbait, plus Garam and Tandoori masalas as the powdered additives. This really did the business, and I went out expecting to catch roach over 1lb. Invariably I did, too. Some of the bites were amazing. With no warning the tip would go round a good two feet, like lightning, lifting the rod out of the rests. Unmissable bites - but I missed half of them. These bites ripped the maggots from the hook, leaving me scratching my head, while the ones I landed hooked themselves anyway. It took me some time to work out what was happening.

Who says I've lost my bottle? You tend to accumulate this sort of collection when you get into the specialist bait game!

Roach on the Trent do not fall regularly to the feeder, and even when float fishing it can take an hour or more of regular feeding before the better fish start to show. After an hour with my feeder tactics the swim is usually full of fish, and when the roach can no longer resist the flavour attraction they have to dash in quick to beat the bream and skimmers. Wallop! Not all the bites were like this, though. Sometimes it was just the normal tap-tap on the quiver, but whenever I had one of those rod-wrenchers it was always a roach in excess of 1lb, and often 1lb 8oz or more. It was to be another two years before I sorted out a method of taming these bites, of which more later.

Meanwhile I was taking tremendous catches, even topping 50lb whenever I had a full day to spare. This wasn't very often, thanks to work, the curse of the fishing classes, but I could not complain. Roach, chub, perch, bream, carp, skimmers, hybrids, gudgeon, even bleak and eels came my way as I zinged happily through the winter, and I also found a way to increase my fishing time. I had tried to catch the Trent roach in the winter darkness in my Clumber Park days, but they would not have it. I knew bream and chub would, though, and I found my whole season had altered. I fished two or three evenings a week, after tea, as I often did in summer, and caught just as many fish. I even stayed until 1 a.m. one February night, and the fish were still feeding when I left.

I let one other friend into the "hot" maggot secret, and he took it to a well-known Trent chub swim and really showed me how it was done. Two hundred and eighteen pounds of chub from 1lb 8oz to 3lb 8oz! That's some catch!

I had a change one day and took the Zing feeder to a notoriously hard stretch of the upper Derbyshire Derwent, which is known for its handful of good chub, and very little else. I got bites all right - minnows, six solid hours of them. Finally, in the last hour, I had a chub, but what a belter at 4lb 11oz. After that trip the bad weather really came, with high, dirty and icy cold water. It was one of the few times that I have recorded the Trent running below 40 degrees F., yet I still caught fish. I did not get the fabulous warm water bags, of course, but on a river which was totally out of sorts I had 10lb, 20lb and 30lb catches while everyone else I could see was struggling for bites. Summer, winter, warm water or cold, I could keep catching. It couldn't get much better, could it?

I spent the following close season almost jumping up and down, waiting for the off. With my new Red Zing I was going to murder them, but on the opening night I fell flat on my face. I had broken my own ground rules, and gone without any alternative baits. Armed only with the "hot" maggots it was my turn to endure what had become a totally unfamiliar situation - a struggle for bites, while all around me they were catching. The flavour was totally unsuitable for the Trent at 70 degrees F. and above, but it was a failure which both teaches a valuable lesson and demonstrates that flavours actually work - if you get them right. The resounding message from that trip was that fish do react positively and negatively. If they did not I would not have scored so often when I had it right, and I would not have been hammered out of sight on opening night. "Hot" baits in hot weather did not work on the Trent; it was a vital discovery.

I went back to paste baits for a few more trips, and had the fish queuing up again, but for some reason the glitter had gone off. I felt I needed a change so I went back to my reservoir, to learn more important lessons. For example the Zing did work there in summer, though of course the temperature was not as high as it was on the artificially warmed River Trent. It illustrates the point that you have to get it right for each venue. I ditched Zing in favour of other flavours, trying all the time to expand my knowledge. Aniseed (by no means a new flavour!), Durian, Maplecream, Freshwater Mussel, Vanilla... they all worked, though some clearly better than others, and new patterns began to emerge.

Sometimes all the bigger reservoir fish fell to one particular flavour, while the other rod produced just as many, but smaller fish, on another flavour. That could change again, next time out, if the water had cooled a couple of degrees, or I faced a calm day rather than a windy one. The questions were piling up, and my mind was going into a spin. Did the strength of light influence their preference for a flavour? What about the depth? Strength of wind? Did a temperature change of as little as one degree make a difference? All I could do was record everything carefully, and try to make sense of it all in the next close season. By the end of that summer, however, at least one important fact was emerging - get the flavour right and the *bigger* fish of a given species could be attracted. This raised a whole new set of possibilities, and when results slowed at the reservoir with the onset of autumn I returned again to the Trent, with renewed enthusiasm.

As luck would have it my first weekend coincided with a rapidly rising and dirty river, which killed sport stone dead. All along the stretch anglers were blanking, and I felt really dubious about trying a new approach in such conditions. I had decided on Garlic flavoured maggots, with garlic powder in the groundbait, but like everyone else I struggled. I had only one bite during a Saturday afternoon session of three hours' 30 minutes, but it turned out to be a small common carp of 2lb 8oz. I would have called it pure luck, except that the following day I had only one bite again, in five hours, from a common carp weighing 6lb. I knew enough by now not to accept this as a coincidence, but subsequent trips with Garlic, in low water, brought just the usual roach, bream and species other than carp. I marked Garlic down as a coloured water carp flavour, but it was to be several years before I followed up on it - with unexpected results.

I had heard that Nutrabaits had produced a very potent garlic flavour, so I set off for my nearest tackle shop to get some. I searched the shelves, but although practically every other flavour was for sale there was no sign of garlic. When I inquired at the counter the lady

A bag of quality perch to 1lb 12oz, from the River Trent.

assistant's face just blanched. "Oh, no! Not that one, please!" When I insisted she explained that it was now kept outside, ever since an angler had opened a bottle in the shop. The staff had immediately gone on strike, and all the customers had walked out. It seemed promising! She took some persuading to go out and fetch me one of the offending bottles, returning with it in a brown paper bag, held at arm's length! I later found that inside the bag there was a sealed, thick plastic bag, inside which was a sealed plastic tub, inside which was a heavy duty glass bottle which held the garlic. And it still left the car reeking on the short drive back home.

I took it straight down to the shed, but my wife was sniffing suspiciously, and glaring at me, the moment I entered the house. Before I could finish explaining she was packing her bags, so I had to admit defeat. The garlic still sits there to this day, banished to the far corner of the shed, and even the flies won't go near it. To be honest it really is evil, but perhaps I will try it some time - after the divorce...

For some time rumours had been reaching me about big Trent perch, a fish for which I had always had a special affection. Affection? I have to admit that all fish are special to me. Over the years I have had a fling with eels, tench, chub, grayling, carp, roach, crucians, pike... just about all of them, and at the time every one of them has been special. I understand the dedication of the single species man, for I have been there myself, but he really does miss out on so much.

Back in the sixties I fished for perch quite seriously, and was as upset as anyone when disease all but wiped them out. Now, with reports of two-pounders from all along the river, and the one-pounders I had been picking up on the feeder, the old feelings began to stir. It was time to have a proper try for them.

I decided to fish an area of what is known as the upper Trent. Here I had a smaller, narrower river, with far fewer bream but a lot more chub and barbel. It is very much like the Trent used to be in days of yore, twisting and turning, with gravelly runs everywhere and, best of all, no boat traffic. Scattered among those fast runs are quiet corners, bays, pools and plenty of overhanging willows. I considered these quieter spots in areas of lively water would be easier to tackle than the long deep stretches of slower water, where the perch could be anywhere.

The first swim I chose was a lovely eddy which swung around and travelled in the opposite direction to the main current for a few yards before gliding under a half-submerged willow. Dropping my feeder by the outer branches of the tree left me with a virtually slack line, due to the two opposing currents almost cancelling each other out. I used the lightest feeder I had, convinced that I would get as many drop-backs as other kinds of bite. I started with the Zing, on a mild November day, and was immediately into fish - small roach, chub, bleak, gudgeon, bite after bite, all day long, and many of them *were* drop-backs. I did catch some perch, six of them, but they were all under 8oz. This needed a re-think...

Next time out I tried a different flavour, Freshwater Mussel, which is based on a natural extract rather than chemicals. I felt it might be more suitable for predators, and it certainly was - chub-type predators! They were better fish than before, too, at around 2lb, and I also had some sizeable roach and a very nice perch weighing 1lb 14oz. This was more like it, but still not very selective, so I really started to ring the changes with the flavours. I even tried a prawn-flavoured powder on the maggots, and got two perch around 1lb 12oz each. On the same day I took a friend who fished the other side of the willow on the Zing. He had four small carp to 4lb 8oz in his catch, but no perch at all.

More evidence of different flavours attracting different species, as we were only 20 yards apart. As the winter went by I delved much further into other powdered flavours, not instead of liquids but as well as. Typical examples were the following, added to each pint of maggots:

5ml *Savoury Meat* to teaspoon of *Feather Meal*
5ml *Pukka Salmon* to teaspoon of *Sardine Meal*
5ml *Curry* to teaspoon of *Garam Masala*
5ml *Hemp* to teaspoon of *Tandoori Masala*
5ml *Garlic* to teaspoon of *Garlic Powder*

They all caught masses of fish, and in among them were the perch I wanted. Over the winter a run of good perch came my way, grand fish to 2lb 13oz, but the highlight was a real beauty of 3lb 2oz (see photograph on the following page). My diaries say that Hemp and Curry flavours were the most successful for big perch, but I felt they just happened to be right on the day. Constantly alternating wet and dry spells meant I never knew what the river would be like until I got there. The temperature fluctuated wildly, the river went up and down and the water varied from clear to very dirty. I caught in all conditions but could feel it in my bones, sometimes, that I was fishing with the wrong flavour. Nevertheless I had proved to my own satisfaction that I could attract the fish I wanted, and even the size I wanted, which opened up all sorts of possibilities. If pushed I would say that for Trent perch the Curry flavour seemed best overall, added to the groundbait water as well as to the maggots and in conjunction with 1oz of Garam Masala to each pint of groundbait.

In recent years the Trent perch fishing has come on in leaps and bounds. There are many swims where it is possible to catch large bags of fish in the 4 to 12oz range, much the same as it was with the chub some years ago. Of even more interest is the size the perch are capable of reaching. I know of several genuine four-pounders, with a biggest of 4lb 10oz, which was, in fact, taken by feeder tactics. Maybe I can find a flavour which will attract only perch over 4lb; I am sure it would not be impossible. At the time I was mentally digesting all this something entirely different came up and set me off on a new tack. No, not a knock-out new flavour, but a different style of fishing where I didn't even need to strike. Since you might like a break from baits and flavours, before it gets more advanced, perhaps I should deal with that now.

The best fish of the perch campaign - a 3lb 2oz specimen which popped out for a curry!

63

UPSTREAM FEEDER FISHING

I can't quite remember how the subject came up, but I was pike
fishing with Colin Dyson at the time. It may have been a mention of
missing bites on the feeder, and Colin gave a quiet sort of smile.
"There's a way of not missing any, Arch," he said, and he came out
with a mind-boggling description of a method which was then on the
secret list, and about which very little has been written, even now. It
was such a way-out concept I did not take him seriously at the time,
and did not even try it until I was suffering an unusually slow session
on the Trent one Sunday.

Colin told me that the method had been developed by the matchman
Bob Roberts, who in turn had adapted something he had read in a Tom
Pickering feature in Coarse Angler magazine. It was so deadly it was
kept under wraps for quite a while, but it all sounded too good to be
true.

According to Colin the method in the match fishing context was to
sit a yard below the peg and cast in a yard upstream of the peg with a
feeder so precisely balanced with lead that it would only just hold in
the flow. The lead was adjusted so finely that even the subtraction of
one swanshot should make the feeder roll in the current (Fig. 23). Colin
had field-tested the idea on the tidal Trent, where the flow alters all the
time, so it was a constant battle to keep the weight properly adjusted.

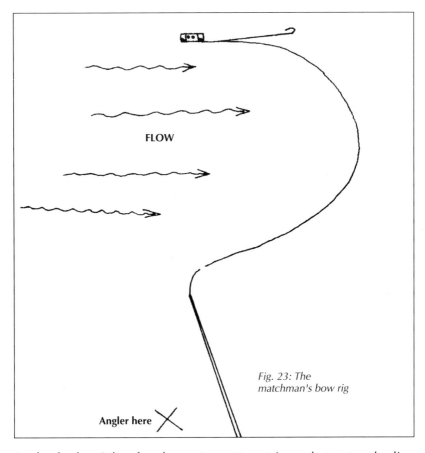

FLOW

Fig. 23: The matchman's bow rig

Angler here ✕

As the feeder sinks after the cast no attempt is made to stop the line coming off the spool, so that by the time the feeder has hit the deck somewhere in front or probably just downstream of the angler, a large bow has developed in the line. No attempt is made to control it; indeed, on some days even more line is actually fed to the feeder.

I can hear you asking how on earth a bite could register, and the same thought crossed my mind as I listened. "You can only get drop-back bites," he said. "Imagine a fish working its way upstream and picking up the bait. Usually it will turn as it does so, dislodging the feeder. Whichever way it swims after taking the bait it eventually has to move the feeder. The bite registers as a constant waggling on the quivertip as the feeder rolls down with the flow, and all you do then is reel in. There is no need to strike, and with that big bow still there it would be pointless anyway. For some reason the fish either don't feel the resistance, because the feeder is rolling with the current, or they do feel something but can't spit the bait out. Anywhere from the 10th to the 20th turn of the reel handle you will feel you have a fish on. It could be anything from a willow blade bream to a great big chub. You want some examples of how well it works?"

He went on to regale me with a tale of a catch of bream so large on the tidal Trent he did not even attempt to lift it over the rocks, but reckoned it was 75lb minimum, possibly over 100lb. A close pal he had merely described the method to the night before had gone out and finished second in a 220-peg match, and would have won it if he had fished it just once in practice. It took him an hour to sort out some of the finer points and he lost by a whisker to a vastly experienced leger man at the next peg. A week later the same angler won a club match with 27lb of bream, and Colin himself beat all but one in a classy field with a big catch of fish which were so small that nobody believed he had done it on the feeder.

With information like that from an impeccable source I should have listened harder, and tried it sooner, for it was ultimately to change my feeder fishing life! As it was I forgot most of what Colin had said until that slow Sunday on the Trent. I do not generally choose to fish this river on a Sunday, mainly because is is the busiest day and the worst of the week for catches, thanks to the weekend power station slowdown which usually results in a marked reduction in water temperature and a corresponding drop in sport. So, more out of boredom than anything, I cast upstream. I immediately noticed how much further out I could hold by doing this. Obviously the feeder was now too heavy for the method as Colin had described it, and on winding in I found the maggots crushed. I had not seen the bite at all.

Next time I went equipped with some lighter feeders, and tried again, and although I was still a bit too heavy I did catch a few fish. The bites showed as a series of small drop-backs on the tip, and rapid winding in produced a fish every two casts. Hardly a feeder-fishing revolution, but I sensed there was something special here, so I really got down to it.

I bought the cheapest feeders I could find, stripped off their thin lead strips and taped or glued them to my favourite Thameslys. I made up a series of these light feeders, ranging in weight from a quarter ounce to threequarters. Having found the one which was best for the swim, i.e. the one which could not quite hold bottom in the flow, I could then fine-tune it. This was done by adding swanshots to the link line until it

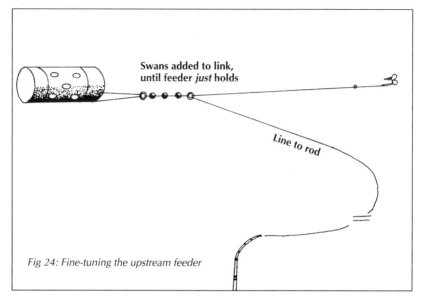

**Swans added to link,
until feeder *just* holds**

Line to rod

Fig 24: Fine-tuning the upstream feeder

just held bottom (Fig 24). The feeder was cast upstream of where I was sitting, and plenty of slack line was fed through the rings after it had settled. When the current took up all the slack the line was hanging almost straight down from the rod tip, rather than pointing upstream.

Colin had said the tip just wagged when the feeder was dislodged. It does in fast water, but in the swim I was fishing it just sprang straight. This really was the business. When the tip straightened I just picked up the rod and wound in. Sure enough I would find a fish attached, four times out of five. Bearing in mind that for the purposes of sorting out the method I had deliberately chosen deep, slow swims, with plenty of small fish available, and that I was still using my strong tackle and big hooks, it was a remarkable success rate. And the bigger the fish are, the better it seems to work. Second time out with the method I caught a 7lb carp, which gave me no problems. Colin had assumed that the success of the "self-hooking" approach depended on the use of small and very sharp hooks, but here I was hooking almost everything on a 14 tied to 3.6lb line!

All too soon the season was ending again, and it arrived before I had completely sorted out the new method. At least it gave me something to think about in the next 13 weeks. I still couldn't quite believe what had been happening. I had been catching simply by winding in a slack line, but why did those fish just hang on and wait for me? They weren't naive Irish fish, but crafty specimens from one of the hardest-fished rivers in Europe. They wouldn't hang on if they knew they were in trouble, so the answer had to be what Colin had suggested - they <u>couldn't</u> let go. But why? To find out I had to imagine what happened with a normal downstream feeder, and I worked it out like this. A fish approaches the bait, picks it up and either drops downstream with it, or downstream and to one side. The hook length has been straightened out by the flow, and is anchored by the feeder. The line is held under tension by the current all the way to the rod top, and there is no slack at all. A wary fish, like a chub, takes a cautious tweak at the bait, detects the drag and immediately ejects. All the angler sees is a little tap on the tip, which he puts down to tiddlers. The less intelligent bream and smaller fish hang on a bit longer, so the tip goes round a bit more.

However, the longer a fish hangs on and the further it moves, the more the tension increases. Everything is conspiring to pull the bait out of the fishes mouth, and it is then that the angler strikes. Unless the hook is well inside the mouth it just comes flying out. The fish could even be lightly pricked, but the impact of the strike flips the hook out without the angler feeling anything. Fisherman and fish are both trying to propel the hook in the same direction! With roach it is even worse, for they bite so much faster. Many of them have ejected the hook before the strike is made. The more logically we look at downstream feeder fishing the more remarkable it is that we catch anything at all.

On the other hand, consider the upstream rig. That wary chub feels the initial resistance, but the lightly balanced feeder has already moved, reducing the drag. He glides away downstream, but the feeder is following him, and we are now involved in the principle that it takes more effort to start something moving than to keep it moving. The hook may be lightly lodged, but the fish cannot eject it, because there is no tension on the line to help it. The fish may not even be trying to eject anyway, because it is now feeling nothing untoward. No matter. If it is trying to eject it can't, and if it isn't trying the situation for the angler is exactly the same. When he takes up slack and makes contact the initial tightening up comes from downstream of the fish, pulling the hook <u>into</u> its mouth, not upstream and out of it.

No wonder the method is so utterly deadly, when you get it right. Think of the more easily foolable bream. They have almost no chance of avoiding such a subtle trap, and it is so effective that even the fast-biting roach have no answer to it either. No wonder Colin had said:

"It's so deadly, Arch, that I am wondering whether it really qualifies as proper fishing."

I understand what he meant, and it is a legitimate point to make. If we caught a fish every cast it would not seem quite right, but we are victims of our own ingenuity. The aim in float fishing is to hit everything, and nobody questions it. For years it was a major challenge for leger fishermen to convert the bites into fish on the bank and now, with upstream legering, we are just about there. We cannot turn the clock back, and it would take a real saint to fish in a way he knew was only 50 per cent efficient. I can live with it, but it has to be remembered, of course, that the full efficiency of this method is not available all the time.

Match anglers have to cope with the limits of their peg, though it is fairly well proven now that they can fish upstream even if the feeder is actually downstream. I know that sounds double Dutch, but it is that big bow of line running downstream of the feeder which really matters. Casting upstream while pleasure fishing is anti-social if there is someone in the next peg, so you have to opt for the matchman's solution. I believe, however, that 100 per cent efficiency with the method depends on casting well upstream, which I will return to in a moment.

My thoughts that close season turned to what the ideal rod might be for upstream feeder fishing. After giving it some consideration I ordered a new custom built rod from Terry Eustace - the 30th such rod, according to my wife, who takes an unfriendly interest in such matters. I asked him not to trim the quivertip back to the normal length, as I wanted the most sensitive tip possible. This was because I had been quite surprised how little lead is needed to hold upstream, when a large bow has been fed into the line. I had found I could fish the middle of the Trent quite delicately, something I had not been able to do before. My biggest problem in conditions of low flow had been to get the tip to take on enough of a curve to properly show the drop-back bites. The use of lighter feeders also meant that a finer tip would be durable enough to withstand the casting.

Without the confinements of a match peg, and with nobody in the upstream swim, I had no reason to cast in front of me, and I began the new season casting upstream about 20 yards. When the feeder hit bottom I would then feed another 15 to 20 yards through the rod rings, and the resultant bow swung way downstream. In fact, when it all tightened up with the flow my quivertip was actually pointing

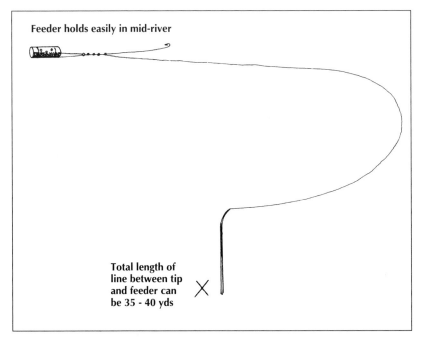

Feeder holds easily in mid-river

Total length of
line between tip
and feeder can
be 35 - 40 yds

Fig. 25: This is how I fish my upstream rig.

downstream (see Fig. 25). In spite of all that had happened with my feeder fishing in the previous few years this new set-up brought some amazing results. Although most of the time there was only about a two inch curve in the quiver I had a variety of bites. A bream, for example, would cause the tip to straighten momentarily, ease back into its curve, straighten again and continue alternating like this, in leisurely manner, until I picked up the rod and wound in. It always took a dozen or more turns of the handle before I felt anything was on. That was one thing every bite had in common, but different species did different things to the tip. The much more energetic roach bite would set the quivertip vibrating as fish and feeder bumped merrily downstream. Bigger fish, like carp or chub, would cause the tip to just straighten suddenly, with no further movement. A little thought produced the reason. These bigger fish would glide away downstream, with feeder following, at a faster pace than the current, leaving the line totally slack and the tip as straight as if there was no tackle attached to it.

It was all so fascinating, and so totally efficient. It did not matter whether the taking fish was a gudgeon, a razor blade bream or a double figure carp. If that tip showed a bite I would wind in a fish. That conversation with Colin Dyson, which I had almost ignored at the time, had solved problems I had battled with for years. At long last I had solved the problem of catching river roach on the rod tip, after 30 years of missing at least half the bites when legering or feedering. Now it was every throw a coconut, and missed bites had become a rarity. No, I have not caught a 2lb Trent roach yet, but I have fished the rig for only two seasons. If a "two" picks up my bait, however, I will catch it; it has become that simple.

I have kept the method under wraps for two years, showing nobody. If anyone was watching I would not cast out, and when the occasional angler stopped to chat, as we all do, it was often very funny. All he would see was the bent quivertip of an angler apparently fishing downstream. At the merest tremble of the tip I would casually pick up the rod and wind in a bream, chub or whatever. The onlookers' expressions would vary from puzzled frowns to slack-jawed disbelief!

The one problem with this type of fishing is that it can take a full minute or more from the feeder actually hitting the water to putting the rod back on the rest, the time being spent feeding out the large bow. Sometimes I have had trouble getting it right because a fish had already taken the bait, and was travelling downstream with the feeder. In fact, if you take off those "fine tune" swanshots the tackle will trundle downstream under its own steam. What price a rolling feeder as a new method of fishing? No, I have not tried it yet, but it is feasible, and some are already doing it. Colin tells me he actually explained it at the time he revealed the upstream method. If he did it passed straight over my head, but in conversation since he has described it as a variation of the rolling leger. Get the weight exactly right and the feeder will move and hold, move and hold. The movement registers on the tip in rhythmic fashion, and a bite immediately changes the usual pattern of movement. If you think about it the big bow downstream is taking the feeder in a straight line downstream, whereas a feeder cast downstream can move only across the current, in a much more unnatural manner.

Perhaps I should have tried it before now, but my approach with the special baits and groundbaits has been to draw the fish right to me, and up to now I have done so well at it there has been no need to go looking for them. In the match fishing context, when it is important to plunder a swim for every fish it is worth, it is a tactic which must be worth a try. As I understand match tactics, it can pay to cast further

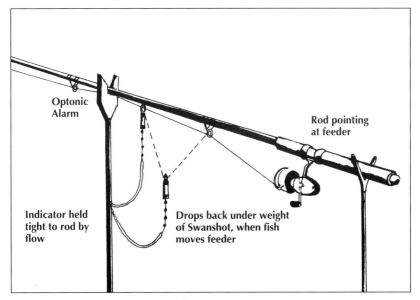

Fig. 26: The drop-back bite set-up for flowing water.

down the swim late in the match to pick up a few bonus fish before the whistle. Do that too soon, though, and it will drive the fish down into the next peg, which isn't wise. Maybe the rolling feeder would be a more subtle intermediate tactic to try.

To return to the matter of the time involved in setting up, it is obviously achieved more quickly in the faster flows, and the faster the flow the more magnified is the effect of a bite on the quiver. In the event of not being able to cast a long way upstream I revert to the matchman's alternative, and often I will dispense with the quivertip altogether. It takes a heavier weight to hold directly in front, and I don't want to risk breaking a quivertip. I just use a normal through-actioned rod instead, and a different but equally effective bite registration system. I fish with an Optonic bite alarm and the hanging bobbin, with at least four swan shots on the retaining line (See Fig. 26). Effectively it is the same rig I described earlier, for Clumber Park, only now the rod is propped high in the air, and the indicator is pulled right up to the rod rings by the flow, despite the weight of the swan shots. This does not matter, because the slightest movement of the feeder will cause it to drop, activating the Optonic. It is a lot easier than peering at the tip for five or six hours, perhaps in strong wind, rain or even dazzling sunshine.

There is one particular type of swim for which the upstream feeder approach is superb, and that's a Trent bridge. Just sit downstream and cast your feeder up into the middle arch, and feed out that big bow. It's easy, and you can fish water which has probably never been fished before. Be prepared for carp and big chub, for both species love such spots.

Bait experiments - and results

All the time I was developing my feeder fishing I was getting feedback from the few friends I had let in on the flavour boom. Colin Dyson went to the tidal Trent and did some stick float fishing with cheese flavoured maggots. One session produced between 30 and 40lb of roach, many of which were over the 1lb mark. He fancied a bit more of that, and went back to the same swim a couple of days later. He had a similar weight, only this time it was all chub, including two he estimated at 5lb plus. He had weighed two at 4-15 for someone in a match the previous weekend, and said they were "markedly smaller" than his brace. Colin, unfortunately, keeps his camera and scales in his specimen hunting kit, and rarely remembers to switch them. He thinks four of his tidal Trent chub were nearer 6lb than 5lb, and since three sixes to 6lb 10oz have been verified in the same area his estimates are not way out of line.

It's an interesting point that all his big chub have fallen to flavoured maggot on 1lb line and size 20 and 22 hooks. When actually trying for them with traditional chub methods (and camera and scales in the bag!) he cannot catch big chub there. Bream, and the occasional carp, yes, but not big chub. Oddly enough, the 6-10 fell to a plug being worked by a pike angler.

Another to score well was Tom Duro, President of the Cotmanhay Angling Club, which controls a prolific stretch of the Erewash Canal in Derbyshire. He amassed large catches of gudgeon on hemp flavoured maggots, while those around him struggled for bites - a vital advantage in a match. He also took several first class roach from this hard-fished water, all over 1lb and up to 1lb 10oz. The bait was simple bread paste flavoured with garlic salt bought from a supermarket. Another successful special paste he developed was peanut butter stiffened with soya flour. Several canal carp fell for that one.

He also told me about catching three small pike on Pukka Salmon flavoured boilies meant for carp. This was yet further evidence that flavours attract pike - remember my reservoir catches on flavoured maggot? - but I have never really considered feeder fishing for them, for the simple reason that pike could simply engulf the feeder. One did just that on the Trent one day, while I was winding in. The feeder was spluttering across the surface very fast when a jack of about 4lb launched itself out of the water, vertically, at least two feet behind the feeder. Executing a neat turnover in mid air it came down straight as an arrow, taking the feeder so neatly I never felt it go. I was left gazing stupidly at a severed line, fluttering in the breeze. Chalk one up to the fish!

At one time I did some fishing with flavoured maize, presenting the bait on the hair rig. Through the summer the various fruity flavours brought me several good chub, but in line with previous experience the results tapered off on the autumn. Changing to curry flavour brought the fish back with a bang, even in dirty water.

All this miscellaneous information was fed into my mental computer, and into my diaries, of course. I carried on experimenting and improving, with the result that my feeder fishing just got better and better. And then, one day, I got a real shock. I was soundly beaten by the angler in the adjoining swim. On my local water! On feeder and maggot! How dare he do such a thing?

It does us all good to lose sometimes, though, and luckily this chap was quite open about his catch. The following story underlines the fact that there is always something else to learn...

The river was high and coloured from recently melted snow, with a temperature of only 39 degrees F. These are absolutely the worst conditions on the River Trent, but I had become used to succeeding in such circumstances when others struggled. I set out for a nice backwater that I knew, but at least 10 other anglers had had the same idea, and got there before me. The best spot was occupied by the angler just mentioned, but as luck would have it the next swim along was being vacated by a chap who had "struggled three hours just for bits."

I got rapidly installed and was soon fishing away with one of my spicy winter flavours. It was pretty slow, but it wasn't long before I was notching up a few small bream and hybrids, the best that could be expected on such a day, or so I thought. It became obvious that I was catching more than the anglers around me, with the exception of my immediate neighbour. For every fish I caught he caught at least four, including some nice roach. In fact, he was catching as if it was a nice sunny day, and not in the icy conditions we were actually enduring. I knew he had the better swim, but the advantage of my additives should have more than evened things up.

I just had to find out what was happening, so I wandered across and had a chat with him. All was revealed. For a start he was using lighter tackle than me, an 18 hook to a 1.7lb bottom, and I have to concede that in such conditions it is an advantage. I won't use it myself because I am always hoping for that bigger fish, but on that day it was right. He was also using a FLAVOUR! He had bought a small bottle of Catchum Banana, and was really ladling it onto his maggots. "It seems to keep losing its smell," he said, "so I pop a bit more on now and again. It's right good stuff, you know..."

As he spoke he happily filled the bottle cap and tipped it into his steadily decreasing tin of maggots. I worked out he had used at least 30mls on just two pints, a ridiculously high level. Ridiculous? It was obviously working for him at the time, but I have never gone to that high level myself. I did once dip the baited hook directly into a bottle of Red Zing, and succeeded in bringing my bites to an abrupt halt, but they soon came back when I reverted to maggots which had been treated at the rate of 5mls to the pint. There is clearly an upper limit, but my new friend had not exceeded it. Perhaps it was because Banana is a much more gentle flavour then Zing that more can be used? Whatever, a bottle of Banana now resides on my shelf, along with dozens of others. It was the first fruit flavour I had known to work in winter, but maybe this incident gives us another clue. Upping the levels may work in winter, but I have yet to test that theory.

Perhaps now is a good time to list all the liquid flavours which have caught fish for me, along with the name of the firms which produce them. Remember that a Strawberry from one company is not necessarily the same as Strawberry from another. Here goes:

NUTRABAITS

Geranium Oil	*Geranium Terpennes*
Garlic Oil	*Black Pepper Oil*

ROD HUTCHINSON PRODUCTS

Sense Appeal	*Regular Sense Appeal*
Savoury Sense Appeal	*Spice Sense Appeal*

Shellfish Sense Appeal	*Vanilla Bean*
Scopex	*Maple Creme*
Ultraspice	*Megaspice*
Lugworm and Crab	*Coffee Creme*
Chocolate Malt	*Mango and Pineapple*
Sweet Mango	*Crayfish*
Freshwater Mussel	*Banana*
Strawberry Dream	*Bramble Jelly*

CATCHUM 88

Blackcurrant	*Durian*
Florentine A	*Florentine B*
Gorgonzola	*Garlic*
Mulligatawny	*Pungent Spice*
Cockle	*Luncheon Meat*
Pukka Salmon	*Cream*
Fish Spawn	*Caramel*
Seafood	*Savoury Meat*
Vanilla	*Caramel Sense Appeal*
Aquamino	*Strawberry Sense Appeal*
Aquacrave Cherry Top	*Aquacrave Swan Mussel*
Protaste	*Intense Sweetener*
Sweetcorn	*Hemp*
Nectar	*Aniseed*

GEOFF KEMP BAITS

Red Zing

Every one of these has produced fish, either on its own or blended with others. In spite of the complexities of flavoured baits I had learned enough to raise my fishing to undreamed of heights, and I'd had five years of continuous big catches. It was now becoming very familiar; if I went feeder fishing I would catch a lot of fish, and the question had to be asked. Just how many more big bags did I need to catch? I was getting stale, and badly in need of a new challenge. One was round the corner...

THE RUDD PIT

An angling pal of mine for many years, pipe-smoking Albert Whittle, had often enthused over a good catch of rudd he had once made, and why didn't we have a crack at them some time? After all, his biggest fish had gone a good 3lbs. I had always tried to point out that it had been about 12 years ago, and the place would have changed. Probably the fish had long since died, but nothing would convince Albert. The only way to shut him up was to try it, and all of a sudden the prospect became quite interesting. I hadn't even seen a rudd for many years, and they are among the most beautiful of fish.

I knew the gravel pit in question was hardly ever fished, due to the fact that it had a reputation for being difficult. The once-yearly match by the controlling club had just proved the point - one tench and a string of dry nets. There is a crazy streak in me; I agreed to have a go.

I fell in love with the place immediately. Surrounded by trees and vegetation covered banks, it had an air of neglect I found somehow refreshing. I even had to cut back the brambles before I could fish - a far cry from the well-trodden Trent swims I had been haunting for so long. The pit covered about three acres, and had a single gravel spit running out into it for about 20 feet. To one side there was shallow water, with deeper water on the other. The spit of land was just three feet wide, and it seemed an obvious place to fish. Over the next two years, did I but know it, I was destined to spend nearly ninety evenings

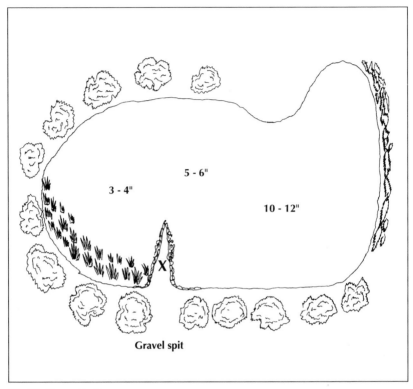

Fig. 27: The rudd pit.

there, plus a couple of mornings. The map (Fig. 27) gives you some idea of the geography of the place. Some of you may recognise it, but do not bother to seek it out, for reasons which will become clear a bit later.

The first session I spent there with Albert we both sat on the spit, each with float-fished maggots in the shallows and a feeder rod fished in the deeps. We blanked. Worse still, we did not see any signs of fish; no rolls, no swirls. The place seemed dead. Could it be as bad as legend had it? Two days later we returned, and blanked again, and once more the water seemed devoid of life. Obviously this was not going to be easy, even with our modern armoury of flavours and additives, so it was time to get down to some proper spadework.

On the next trip I spent the first two hours with the depthometer, the float and an Arlesey bomb before I even tied on a hook. The first two were used to check the depth, the float for the shallows and the depthometer for the deeps. Later the bomb was cast all around the spit, and retrieved slowly. Gravel can clearly be felt, as can silt and soft mud, and with a bit of effort a surprisingly good picture of the make-up of the bottom can be gained. To the left the depth was about 3ft 6in., shelving slowly away from the spit, and it had a very soft and silty bottom. Not surprisingly there was a lot of weed in this area. To the right it was 10ft deep with a hard, gravel bottom, covered by a thin layer of silt.

The two totally different areas only feet apart puzzled me, until I had a chat with one of the workmen. This was still a working complex, with sand and gravel being washed clean daily, and the resulting sediment was filtered into another large pit just behind me. This was evidenced by the huge area of silty sand which now covered a good half of that 20 acre water. Apparently a few years previously this sediment had been diverted into the rudd pit, which rapidly filled up the left half of it. It was prevented from spreading further by the spit we were fishing from. Fortunately the sludge had soon been diverted back into the large pit. This slow filling was a deliberate company policy, as they planned to return the site to the farmer, as grazing land, when it was finally worked out. I also learned that my pit was around 30 years old, so it had had plenty of time to really mature.

The next time out we blanked again, but I did not really mind. It was such a relaxing change from the frenetic activity on the Trent, the scenery was soft and green and the spit faced west into the setting sun, giving me some glorious sunsets to contemplate. I was in no hurry.

Not so Albert. In an effort to speed things up he tried an early morning session, to see if we were missing out. He never had a bite, because another angler had beaten him to the spit - the first time we had seen anyone else there. This angler caught six tench, two of them over 4lbs and a further fish which was a beauty of 6lbs exactly. Now we really sat up and took notice. In spite of the angling weeklies regularly displaying photographs of tench of 7, 8 and 9lb, even 10lbs plus at times, tench of 4lb are fair fish in my locality, and 5lbs is a good one. With tench like these on my doorstep who cared if the rudd had perhaps gone long ago?

All my old enthusiasm came flooding back, and I really got interested again. These fish had all been caught on feeder maggots (the inevitable block end again), and I knew that sooner or later I would find a winning flavour combination. Then an event occurred which kicked me right into top gear. Albert caught a huge rudd.

After seeing those tench he had gone for another early morning session, and got the water to himself. Strangely we saw little more of the other angler, or anyone else for that matter. Could there be a better tench water in the area, which we did not know about? It was mild, wet and windy when Albert fished his second morning, more like November than July, as was so much of that particular early season. Albert quickly set up one rod only, with float tackle, dropping it into the deep water just off the end of his rod. Then he hurriedly retired behind his brolly, to be disturbed by just three bites. The first produced a 3lb tench. The second the large rudd and the third produced the reason why I haunted the place for the better part of two seasons.

The first I knew of all this was when a wet and bedraggled Albert came thumping on my office door at 11 a.m. that Saturday morning. Yes, I have to work Saturdays... When I had calmed him down long enough to make out what he was saying I abandoned the telephone and went haring off to the pit with him, armed with scales, weigh sling and camera. When Albert lifted his net from the water my heart skipped a beat, for there on the mesh lay a rudd which literally shone like a beacon, despite the lowering grey skies. The scales said 3lb 12oz - a monstrous rudd for my neck of the woods - and while the photograph gives some idea of the quality of the fish it would take more eloquence than I can command to accurately describe its living presence.

I felt like I was looking at the Holy Grail itself, but thrilled as Albert was I could sense that something was on his mind. He was not as ecstatic as he should have been, and the reason emerged when he told me of his third bite. It seemed that he had hooked a second rudd, which he played out and had on its side waiting for the landing net. As it touched the rim it gave one last, despairing jerk, and the hook pinged out. When Albert had settled down to talk rationally about the matter he came out with a stunning estimate of its size - "at least half as big again" as the 3lb 12oz fish!

Had it been someone I knew less well I would have reserved judgment, but I knew Albert never exaggerated. All his "3lb 8oz" tench or bream scale over 4lb when I weigh them for him. When he said the fish had been at least half as big again I knew he was talking about a rudd which would have toppled the late Rev. E.C. Alston from the place he had occupied in the record list for over 50 years. Albert had been inches away from doing just that. Much less than half as big again would have taken him past Alston's mark of 4lb 8oz... but we

Albert Whittle's 3lb 12oz rudd. Imagine what the big one looked like!

were still in with a chance, weren't we? What better target for my flavoured feeder rigs?

It was pure coincidence, but at the time the angling weeklies were full of the exploits of a small group of anglers on a Leicestershire reservoir, who had caught some enormous rudd up to 4lb 5oz. They believed the record might go, and I found myself thinking what consternation it would cause if Albert or I beat them to it from an unknown and unsuspected water. We decided to keep Albert's fish under wraps - indeed it has never been publicised until now - until we had either caught the monster or conceded defeat.

It seems almost over the top to mention another event from that rain-soaked morning, but Albert got up at one stage to stretch his legs. In a short walk along the bank he saw what he thought was the outline of a pike of about 8lb, lying in the margin in only a foot of water. As he came alongside it cruised slowly away in full view. It was a giant chub! Over the following summer I did in fact see an occasional good chub glide by, and they were always well over 4lb, but the biggest I saw was perhaps 5lb 8oz. Even the thought of a possible record chub scarcely registered with me, so taken up was I with the vision of that spectacular rudd. It all fitted a well-known pattern, though. Neglected water, small number of big fish... These are precisely the kind of fisheries which do produce record-breakers. They can also break hearts!

To start my campaign in earnest I first went into the literature. I have an extensive library covering all aspects of angling, from the giants of yesteryear, like J.W. Martin, the Trent Otter, right up to the whizz-kids of today, who seem to catch 30lb carp most weekends. In all this wealth of words, however, there was very little about rudd. A few books had short chapters about fishing for them near the surface, or perhaps the taking of large bags in Ireland, but only John Bailey, in his book "In Visible Waters," came close to understanding them. He had spent all of one summer encamped on a Norfolk estate lake, living like the fish. He slept when they slept, moved when they moved, fished when they fed. Fascinating reading, but he had the advantage of being able to observe the fish regularly, and chart their movements. In the two years I spent at my rudd pit I never saw a roll, a swirl or any other sign that these fish even existed.

Colin Dyson made me wonder about some of the authors, for he, too, had tried researching rudd in his Norfolk days. He had concluded that a long succession of authors had borrowed from each other in the days when fishing books covered every species. They all felt the need to include rudd while knowing precious little about them. They all made the point about the underslung mouth being purpose designed for surface feeding, yet almost all his big rudd had been taken in the first hour or so of darkness on legered bread. His biggest, at 3lb 7oz, had slurped a lobworm, cast to what he thought was a carp, and he was so interested in my rudd pit he made me promise to call him if I caught anything exceptional. He told me the tale of a friend, Ted Grant, who had caught a monstrous rudd which made his 3-7 look small, but he accidentally dropped it back in while showing it to Colin.

"That rudd was well over 4lb, and ever since I have kept the image in my mind," he said. "I want to see a 4lb rudd weighed, and to compare it with the memory of Ted's fish. He talked about that rudd until the day he died, but the most memorable thing he said was that "God had to be on the side of the Rev. Alston." I thought of Albert's similar experience, and concluded that the late Ted Grant might well have been right!

I continued to read my books as I carried on fishing. One rod stayed on the feeder all the time, and I had once again dug out my old Conoflex glass fibre rods, of Clumber Park fame. I could not help thinking of that hook flipping out of the monster rudd, something I had to avoid at all costs. Albert had described the fight as "heavy and jagging," similar to the actions of a big perch, so these soft rods should be ideal. I fished with my standard fixed paternoster, but used the lightest feeders I had. I also reduced the small shot six inches from the hook to a dust shot. This was to compensate for the fine silt on the bottom, and anyway, I had no distance to cast. I felt sure that the slopes of the gravel bar I was sitting on would provide all the features the fish needed, particularly if I baited up that area with my remaining maggots and groundbait each time I left.

Albert's fish had fallen to three red maggots, and I gave some thought to this, but in the end I decided to stick to white. I remember when chrysodine maggots were all the rage, and now that has faded red is the "in" colour. During all that period I had been catching on white maggots, and still do. I firmly believe the flavour is the really decisive factor.

My second rod I float-fished with, trying different baits, and it was this that brought me my first fish one evening, a scrappy tench of just over 4lbs, which fell to a lump of cheese. The weather finally changed that summer, and the pit came to life. We started to see big swirls on the surface, which on investigation proved to be the few large chub which were present. We never did see the giant chub again, neither did we ever catch one of any size, though I did try for quite a long time by baiting one of my rods with sardine. The tactic has brought me good chub many times, but all it produced on this particular water was a regular run of small pike, so I dropped it. With the warmer temperatures the surface started to dimple with small fry, insect life multiplied and the whole water started to show more activity.

In the first half of the summer Albert well and truly showed me the way home. Float-fishing plain maggots in the weedy shallows he caught a second rudd of 2lb 1oz, while I blanked. Not content with that, two days later he took another of 2lb 1oz, again on unflavoured maggots, and again I blanked. To add insult to injury he also had a 4lb tench on his second rod, to a legered lobworm. Both the rudd had fallen to simple laying on tactics. For the first time I began to have doubts about the flavours. Could it be that on this virtually unfished water they were actually deterring the fish? Was I trying to use a sledgehammer to crack a nut? With my confidence dented I sneaked back to the Trent, but immediately the fish were queuing up again. There had to be an answer, and luckily there was.

I found an article in one of the specialist magazines by a carp angler who was trying out a new range of flavours described as "essential oils" by Nutrabaits. Evidently there were no man-made chemicals involved in these. Each oil was based on completely natural products derived from plants and vegetables etc, and the one which caught my eye was Geranium Oil, which is obtained by crushing the leaves of the geranium plant. The carp angler had mixed some of this into a soft paste, and thrown it into his local lake to see what happened. Immediately roach and rudd had come swarming out of the depths onto the shallows, and they devoured the paste in no time.

Within 48 hours I had obtained this flavour, which was so strong it came supplied with a dropper so you can actually measure it out drop by drop. I started by squeezing eight drops into each pint of maggots, plus 10 drops into the water needed for two pints of groundbait. And it worked! First time out I had a tench of 4lb 2oz, and lost a decidedly heavier one which went with power and speed into the weeds. Both took three maggots on a 14 hook to 3.6lb line. It was Albert's turn to blank.

Two nights later I had a real baby of a tench at 2lbs, while Albert chipped in with one of 4lb 8oz on the lobworm. More important, little fish showed for the first time. I took four small perch and two roach, none as big as 4oz. This proved that not only was the flavour working, but so was the usual fixed paternoster. I had no shots at all on the indicator, due to the short range at which I was fishing, and its own weight was just enough to hold the line taut to the feeder. It was extremely sensitive, and even the little fish had given good bites.

I caught yet again on the following trip, another tench of 3lb 9oz plus another half dozen small roach and perch. From then on I abandoned the float rod, and for the rest of my time on the pit I concentrated on two feeder rods. Meanwhile Albert came up with another tench on lobworm, a real belter of 6lbs. Things were looking up.

There followed, however, a two-week blank for both of us. The weather turned hot and sunny, coupled with no wind and a moon at nights. These conditions have always been the kiss of death on stillwaters, and even my feeder/flavour techniques could not alter that. So I tried an early morning, and this gave me two beautiful tench of 4lb 13oz and 5lb 11oz in the first hour of daylight. Nice fish, but not what

A brace of nice tench from the rudd pit - 4lb 13oz and 5lb 11oz

I was looking for. Those last two rudd of Albert's had been taken in the falling light, and I felt certain that was the best time, despite the regular blanks.

I had started to worry about that silty bottom, as I felt the maggots could be rapidly dispersing into it. Even the hook bait might be partially obscured some of the time. I was by now using a no. 12 hook to 4.6lb line as standard because of the terrific pulling power of those tench, so I decided to swap one of the three maggots for a caster. Being slightly more buoyant, it could help. On the other rod I tried pinching a piece of bread flake to the shank of the hook, for the same reason. Both approaches seemed to work, for I caught a couple more tench to just over 4lbs. Albert came up with another good one of 5lb 14oz, on two maggots and a caster, Maple Creme flavoured, but overall the fishing remained very slow.

It was now mid-August, and I had been fishing the water for four or five evenings a week from the start of the season. As a quest for rudd it had been singularly unsuccessful, for I had not yet caught one. My luck was about to change, however, for the weather turned windy and much cooler. It gave the pit a new lease of life, for on the first trip in the changed conditions Albert produced yet another rudd weighing 2lb 1oz, and I had one weighing 1lb 14oz, just after dark. It was the first to be taken in full darkness. The next evening I was back again, and had another rudd of 2lbs exactly. I was starting to get excited - three rudd in a week, and mine were the biggest I had ever caught in more than 30 years of angling.

I was generally fishing from 6 p.m. to 11 p.m., taking just one pint of maggots, two pints of groundbait, a few casters and a slice of bread. Anything left over was chucked in the swim when I left, so I was probably baiting up with four pints of maggots and eight pints of groundbait per week. Whether it was this, or the slowly changing season which had brought the fish on, I do not know, but my faith in the feeder approach was finally paying off.

Then, of course, it dried up on me again. We went into another slow patch which became so bad that Albert lost interest, and drifted back to the Trent. With a 3lb 12oz rudd and a 6lb tench to his credit who could blame him, but I was still fired up by the memory of his 3-12 and Albert's account of the one that got away. I grimly soldiered on, getting odd tench, small roach and perch and the inevitable blanks. In desperation I tried a change of flavour on one of the rods, the old favourite Hemp on the bait and groundbait. It produced three bites the first time I tried it - a tench of 1lb 12oz, a rudd of 1lb 14oz and, after dark, a mighty tench of 7lb 10oz. When I started fishing such a tench would have broken the national record, and many areas of the country, including mine, are still in much the same time warp. There has perhaps been some increase in the size of tench nationally, but the spectacular increases have taken place in relatively few areas. Not too many anglers have topped 7lbs in Nottinghamshire, and fewer still have caught them after they have shed their spawn. I was naturally ecstatic - but not too excited to realise that I had learned another valuable lesson.

It was further proof that the tastes of the fish change with the season, and never again did I use the same flavour on both rods at the same time. The bait had still been two maggots and a caster, and I could not wait to get there again. There followed three total blanks, but then came two rudd in one evening. One came immediately, before the second rod was set up, and weighed 2lb 3oz. The other came just on dusk, and weighed 1lb 14oz. Both fell to the Hemp, with Garam

Masala in the groundbait.

After the big tench I had stepped up the tackle again, tying the no. 12 to a 6.5lb Ultima hook link, but those rudd had taken the baits without hesitation. One recurring theme in what little has been written about rudd is that they are not particularly tackle shy, and that is borne out by my experience. All the rudd I had caught thus far had taken the baits well inside their mouths, and all needed the disgorger.

September arrived, and now I concentrated even harder. So often this proves to be the key time of the year on stillwaters, for with the shorter evenings much less time is spent waiting for the sunset. The vital two hours after dark come sooner, but in spite of this I went through another period of struggle - more blanks, punctuated by the odd tench to nearly 5lbs and several more roach and perch. Then, in late September, I clicked for exactly the right kind of night - warm, cloudy and with a slight breeze. I had four small tench in quick succession, from 1lb 12oz to 2lb 4oz, and then a sailaway bite connected me with a heavy, thumping fish.

When it first surfaced in the fading light I actually started to tremble. It was not the fish, but at 3lb 3oz it was a tremendous rudd. With the torchlight reflecting from its flanks it looked magnificent; almost unreal. I actually wanted to keep it, to own it, and it was a real wrench to put it back. For the record, it had taken the maggot/caster combination, with Hemp and Garam Masala, the same as the biggest tench. The following night I had another rudd of exactly 2lbs, the only difference in method being that the caster had been replaced with a pinch of bread flake.

Now it was October, and the game was as good as over. I caught a few more tench to 4lb 12oz but no rudd. The weather broke early in the month and the water temperature fell rapidly. After six biteless sessions I abandoned it for that season, though I did have just one more fruitless trip in November.

So what had I done? I'd had eight rudd from 1lb 14oz to 3lb 3oz, each one bigger than any I had caught in the past, and I had landed more than 40 tench, including my best to date. I had made the feeder approach work on a far from easy water, and succeeded with a new type of flavour, the oil-based Geranium. I had also established that there were two groups of rudd - those a few ounces either side of 2lb and just a tiny few in excess of 3lbs, up to possible record status. So far contact had been made with three of that group, my 3lb 3oz fish, Albert's 3-12 and the lost monster. Perhaps that was all that was there?

*The 3lb 3oz rudd,
which fell to a
Hemp-flavoured
and spicy bait.*

On the debit side I had suffered so many blanks, so many wasted hours, but I felt there was so much more I could do. I resolved that before the next season came around I would locate and read everything which had been written about flavours and additives, if that was humanly possible. I already knew a lot, but over the previous two or three years developments on the carp scene had surged ahead, and there was so much more to learn.

Specialist bait suppliers were springing up all over the place, each of them producing new catalogues each year. Some of the names they came up with! Enhancers, Cajolers, Arousers, Stimulators... Were these to do with baits, or were they goodies from a sex shop? After weeks of study I decided to retain or add the following to my bait armoury for the coming season:

OIL-BASED FLAVOURS

The Geranium had been such a success (although no more so than the alcohol-based Hemp) that it certainly warranted further trial.

INTENSE SWEETENER

A concentrated liquid sweetener which does just that.

PROTASTE

A new type of sweetener, sold by Catchum. All flavour firms sell sweeteners, but this is one which is said to enhance any flavour, and to emulsify (thin out) any oil. It certainly smelled different, and very strongly. I decided to use it, but only at very low levels, as I felt it could possibly mask the flavour's own attraction.

SENSE APPEALS

These are what amount to bottles of liquid protein, rich in amino acids and mixed with oils. This is not the sort of book where I need to go deeply into the formulae for such liquids, but the theory is that the flavour draws the fish from a distance, and when they reach the area of the tackle they can detect the Sense Appeal in suspension in the water immediately around the bait. It is almost like the soup before the main course. If it all seems hard to accept just take my word for it; it works! There is a range of flavoured Sense Appeals in addition to the Regular - Spice, Savoury, Fish, etc - which can be used to match up with your chosen flavour.

AQUACRAVE, AQUAMINO, NUTRAMINO, MINAMINO

Basically these are also protein in liquid form again, but without added oils, so they are much more watery. They are also very expensive. They mix nicely with flavours, which helps to give them added food value, and if you are wealthy enough you can even add them to your groundbait. Some of them have a small amount of flavour added, such as Aquacrave Cherry Top and Aquacrave Swan Mussel, so they can be used on their own or blended with matching flavours. In case this is getting confusing I have detailed how I use these liquid proteins later in this chapter.

APPETITE STIMULATORS

These are all powders, rather than liquids, and they are a taste rather than a smell. In other words they do not do any fish attracting, but once the fish has actually mouthed them their taste buds are stimulated, making them want some more. They are ideal for adding to your pastes at just a level teaspoonful per loaf, and even better for adding to groundbait. I use a teaspoon to each three pints of dry mix. The stimulators come in various tastes, meat, fish, sweet etc, so again you can match them up to the flavour of your choice.

BLENDS

The carp anglers have proved beyond doubt that blending two or more liquids together can actually produce better results than either flavour on its own. So, if you have been struggling to follow me so far, consider this. I have covered two or three dozen only, up to here, but the specialist catalogues list two or three hundred. The possible combinations of two or more together runs into millions. It would take a mathematical genius to work it out.

It means, of course, that if you can find a blend which works there is every chance that it will remain uniquely yours, but before your brain bogs down completely let me make a suggestion. You cannot reach the stage I am at by browsing through this book, so save your brain cells and buy it. That way I make a few bob and you can catch me up. Fair enough?

Oh, well, let's get back to the rudd pit. My diary for the previous season had shown up one indisputable fact; the change from one flavour to another (Geranium to Hemp) had brought the fishing back to life, though both liquids had produced a good number of fish. On the river the same thing had happened, but I had put it down to the changing seasons, or the varying water levels and temperatures. Were there far more subtle changes taking place on the pit? Or was it much more simple? Maybe the fish just liked a change, as we do.

June 16, 1989, saw me on the gravel spit with the usual two fixed paternoster set-ups, both with three maggots and a pinch of flake on the hook. That silt bottom still bothered me. On one rod I used Chocolate Malt as the flavour, and Regular Sense Appeal (unflavoured) as the "food value" content. This was applied to the maggots at 5mls and 2.5ml respectively to each pint. The bread/bran groundbait mix had been enhanced by the addition of a teaspoon of Sweet Appetite Stimulator, plus the same combined 7.5mls of flavours to two pints of groundbait mix. The thinking behind the approach was to present a high flavour level, with a low food value back-up.

With the other rod I went the other way, high food value with a low flavour level, using 3mls of Regular Sense Appeal and 3mls of Aquacrave Cherry Top to each pint, plus 10mls of the same mix to two pints of groundbait, along with the teaspoon of Fruit Appetite Stimulator. A lot of trouble? Not really. It only takes a minute to sprinkle two lots of maggots, and not much longer to do groundbait. I have my own Kenwood mixer, and while it is churning the crumb and bran together I slowly tip in the flavoured water. With practice you can produce a superb mix.

That first evening brought me tench of 2lb 14oz, 3lb 4oz and 4lb on the Chocolate Malt set-up, and a good fish of 5lb 13oz to the Cherry Top. Not a bad opener, and a far cry from the early sessions of the previous season. Two days later I was back, but had inadvertently mixed up all my flavours together, so I had to use the same concoction on both rods. I caught a tench of 3lbs and the season's first rudd, weighing 2lbs. Both had taken a mix of Chocolate Malt, Regular Sense Appeal and Aquacrave Cherry Top on the maggots. Now there was something to think about.

Then the weather turned really hot, and the water temperature soared to 78 degrees F. I separated the flavours again and carried on catching despite the wrong conditions. Small roach started to show, and perch (on the 12 hook to 6.5lb line), plus several more tench, including a 5-pounder. Then a strange thing happened. I got three small pike, 2lb 8oz to 3lb 8oz each, all in one session. The night after I had another, plus my hook was bitten off twice; obviously more pike. In fact, before the middle of July I landed nine jacks and lost as many again through bite-offs. Every one fell to the Aquacrave Cherry Top/Sense Appeal combination, so I decided to drop it. I could not expect to catch rudd with such a concentration of pike in the swim, but it speaks volumes about the reaction of fish to flavours.

They stopped coming as soon as I switched flavours, and I did not catch another pike all season. It is one of the reasons why I believe it is possible to find a flavour, or blend of flavours, which will appeal to particular species. Trust me to find one I did not want, but I was only treading the same path as the carp men, decades earlier.

Consistent success on a water which had proved so hard the previous year was further confirmation that the approach was working, for those who want to see it. I was now catching on almost every trip, and last season's run of blanks was just a bad memory. It was obvious that my change of flavours had drastically improved things. The Chocolate Malt mix on the other rod continued to take small roach and perch, plus a steady run of tench, with a satisfying number over 5lbs. In early July I caught my second rudd of the season, at 1lb 14oz, along with tench of 2lb 14oz, 3lb 15oz and 4lb 9oz - great results for just four hours' fishing.

At the end of July the first changes in the pit took place. A petrol-engined pump suddenly appeared on the far side, and it proceeded to take water out to wash gravel from the nearby conveyor belt. It had always happened before, but only from the pit next door. This was now very low, due to heatwave conditions, so I guessed they had decided to rest it and concentrate on my pit. At least they were not channelling the silt residue from these washings back into the pit, for this had reduced the other water to a fraction of its original size over the last few years. Nevertheless the rudd pit began to fall by an inch a day, Monday to Friday, though it regained a little over the weekend when the washing plant closed down.

When I dropped the Cherry Top I replaced it with Scopex, Sense Appeal and Intense Sweetener, at 4mls, 3mls and six drops respectively per pint of maggots. I also added a few drops of Intense Sweetener to the groundbait, along with the same flavours, plus a teaspoon of Sweet Appetite Stimulator. This brought me tench of 5lb 1oz and 5lb 2oz the first time I used it. With yet another demonstration of the effectiveness of a change of flavour I decided to make a change on the other rod as well.

And so it continued throughout that scorching summer, with me ringing the changes with the various flavours more and more often, while the pit level continued to fluctuate like a yo-yo. The table on the right shows some of the combinations used.

The rudd still proved hard to come by, but the few I had were taken on bait no. 5 (two weighing 1lb 12oz and 1lb 15oz), no. 9 (one

MAGGOTS (PER PINT)	GROUNDBAIT (PER 2 PINTS)
1: 3ml Cream, 1ml Aquamino , 1ml Intense Sweetener	Teaspoon Sweet Appetite Stimulator; 5ml Cream
2: 3ml Clove Spice E.A., 2 drops Protaste 2ml Spice Sense Appeal	5ml Spice Sense Appeal Teaspoon Spice Appetite Stimulator
3: 3ml Topper, 3ml Sense Appeal, 6 drops Intense Sweetener	5ml Topper, 1ml Intense Sweetener, teaspoon Fruit Appetite Stimulator
4: 3ml Sweet Mango 3ml Sense Appeal	3ml Intense Sweetener half ounce Lactopro
5: 6 drops Geranium Oil 4ml Spice Sense Appeal 2 drops Protaste	5ml Spice Sense Appeal 2 Drops Geranium Oil teaspoon Spice Appetite Stimulator
6: 6 drops Geranium Oil 4ml Savoury Sense Appeal	6 drops Geranium Oil teaspoon Savoury Appetite Stimulator
7: 5ml Bramble Jelly E.A. 2ml Aquacrave Cherry Top	Teaspoon Fruit Appetite Stimulator , 6 drops Intense Sweetener
8: 3ml Ultraspice 2ml Spice Sense Appeal 5 drops Intense Sweetener	Teaspoon Spice Appetite Stimulator
9: 4 drops Geranium Oil 4ml Sense Appeal 2 drops Protaste	5 drops Geranium Oil teaspoon Spice Appetite Stimulator
10: 3ml Sense Appeal 3ml Aquamino	5ml Aquamino teaspoon Meat Appetite Stimulator

weighing 1lb 14oz) and no. 10 (one of 2lbs)

It is interesting to note that for the second year running Geranium Oil proved a winner, so if you know any fishery holding big rudd it may be worth a try. No. 10 bait was, in fact, a deliberate experiment with no flavours at all; it was just a combination of liquid protein and natural oil extracts. All of the combinations caught tench, roach and perch, and would no doubt have caught more, but in the interests of research I kept moving on to the next one.

I have to say that while I was learning I was also worrying. The fluctuating but steadily shrinking water level filled me with a sense of foreboding, and the gut feeling was that this fascinating fishing, which I had enjoyed almost entirely to myself for the whole summer, might not be mine much longer. All I could do was to go on, feverishly searching for the magic potion which would bring me that giant rudd.

It was not to be. At the end of August I arrived one evening to find the water had a distinct brownish hue, and had a dusty surface film. It did not take long to find the reason why, for the silt channel to the large pit had been blocked up, and re-directed into the shallow corner of the rudd pit. Within two weeks a quarter of the area on the left hand side of the spit had gone, with a smooth surface of sand where once there had been a thick weedbeds.

Initially it did not affect the fishing, in fact the tinge of colour and the loss of some of the feeding area may even have helped. I continued to catch good tench, but although I did not know it at the time I had caught my last rudd. Gradually the weedy shallows vanished under the silt, and the water became more and more murky. There was nothing I could do about it. What price the sadness of the lone angler, when weighed against the interests of a multi-million pound company? By the end of October I had moved back to the Trent, doubting that I would ever fish there again.

In fact I did return the following year. In the back of my mind was the thought that a smaller water, with the natural food choked out of it, should be easy. Maybe that great big rudd would take another bait? I arrived to find that the silt had now completely swallowed the shallow area, and covered my favourite spit with a four inch layer of glutinous quicksand. There was no weed to be found anywhere in the pit, the water of which was now a permanent light brown. I fished one of the remaining swims, and even caught a couple of 3lb tench, but I knew I could not continue.

For me the charm of the place had been destroyed, along with its whole ecology. It was the end of a dream. If only Albert's sudden yearning for another crack at the rudd had swept over him a year or so earlier. If... Life is so full of ifs and buts, missed opportunities, disappointments. God, I reflected, was still on the side of Edward Alston, but the spirit of that great gentleman is surely out there somewhere, willing someone to break his record; knowing, as only he could, what it would mean to someone from the future generations he and others had so inspired. No, Alston would not blame God, or the Devil either. When the inner rage and feelings of futility die away, and we examine these things in a rational way, we cannot vent our fury upon gravel companies for their apparent lapses into vandalism. Look at what they have created for us, the length and breadth of Britain. We have much to thank them for, and must realise that many of the disappointments which we blame them for were pre-ordained by planning laws, and by the ways in which the sand and gravel extractors have to work.

The gravel companies have created much which is permanent; valuable habitats for wild creatures and exciting playgrounds for us, the anglers. Some of what they create is merely transient; here for 10, 20 or even more years. They are wonderful while we have them, and some, by accident of nature, become extra-special. We just have to enjoy them until that pre-ordained day of reckoning comes along, as it inevitably did for my little rudd pit.

I do not grieve for it any more. I just remember what it gave me, and I do not dwell too much upon what else it might have given. The skeleton of Albert's rudd is probably being preserved in the silt which overcame it, but I think I now know something of the excitement Edward Alston must have felt when he discovered how his rudd had grown in that little mere at Thetford. I can also imagine his feelings when the mere dried up. The Lord giveth... and taketh away.

Before my rudd pit was taken away, however, it had one more precious gift to bestow. It was not a great fish; it was better than that. It was the answer to a problem which had plagued me for years, and it was to launch my feeder fishing to new and even dizzier heights. The next chapter heading tells all.

DEAD MAGGOTS

The soft bottom of the rudd pit had always bothered me, but that rapid influx of silt really triggered things off. The sediment in suspension soon settled to the bottom, leaving it covered in a very fine brown mud. This was most noticeable when I retrieved tackle with a pinch of bread flake still on the hook. Most times it would come in almost as if it had been dyed brown on one side, making me wonder what could be happening to the maggots? Experiments in shallow water confirmed the worst; within one minute all the maggots had vanished into the bottom layer. Even the wriggling hookbait managed to half submerge itself, and perhaps totally disappeared in deeper water where the sediment layer might be thicker.

I had always wondered just how effective the feeder maggots really were, particularly at long range, when I could never be entirely sure of the bottom make-up. This is another strong argument for the open-ended feeder, for at least with that you can always be sure of the groundbait remaining near the hook-bait, even when all the loose maggots have vanished. In the past I had abandoned maggots altogether in such circumstances, but now it was nearly October, and my time at the pit was running out. Could anything be done? If only I could keep my bait on the top of the mud I might well catch a lot of fish.

And then I had an idea. Why not try dead maggots? Admittedly they would not wriggle out of the feeder, but a false strike would soon sort that out, and they would certainly stay where I put them. So, how could I kill them? I remembered an experiment I had read about in an article several years ago, by the noted Cheshire bream expert, Graham Marsden. He had worked on similar lines, using boiling water, so I tried this myself. I was not happy with the results. It killed the maggots instantly, but left them looking very different; boiled, in fact! Worse still, it destroyed the flavour with rapid evaporation. I did not think dosing dead maggots with flavours would work, as I had always felt they eat or ingest a certain amount of the flavour, as they do with colour dyes.

The alternative was to freeze them. I put a couple of dozen in a small plastic container and popped them into the deep freeze for half an hour (except that I totally forgot about them and went to bed). When I remembered them next morning they were frozen all right; they rattled around in the container like marbles in a tin! Oh, well, now I would find out how they would be. I certainly did. Two hours later they had thawed out and were wriggling around happily again!

I had probably solved the age-old mystery about what happens to flies in winter, but this did not help me much. Obviously they could stand a lot of frost, far below anything they could expect in the worst of British winters, so next time I gave them a full 24 hours. That did it, and when they softened they were good and dead. They did not look

An unusual River Trent capture. Is it a fully-scaled mirror carp, or an oddball common?

very appetising, I must admit. They had darkened a little, elongated slightly and were very soft, which might not be a bad thing. They looked, though, as if they had not enough juice inside to fill their skins out. On top of that they felt like little strips of cold jelly. I had not realised before just how warm live maggots are.

My next job was to test whether they would hold the flavour, so I treated a full pint of live maggots and sealed them up in a plastic freezer bag for a couple of hours. These bags come on a roll of about 60, complete with plastic ties, and are just the right size to take a pint of maggots. When I considered that the maggots had had enough time to absorb some of the flavour I gave them the deep freeze treatment. At the time I was using a blend of 4ml of Ultraspice, 5 drops of Geranium Oil and 3 drops of Protaste per pint. The reasoning behind this was that the spice and oil flavours complement each other, and the Protaste helps to smooth out the "bite" of the spice, and lightly sweetens the whole blend. Most of my feeder fishing is now done with such blends.

After 24 hours in the freezer, and when thawed out, the dead pint smelled the same as when the maggots were alive, so now I had to put it to the test. Would the fish take such a bait? I thought back to all those years of missed, bites, crushed maggots and the immediate reaction - to change them. Hadn't I read a thousand times that only the liveliest maggots were to be used on the hook? To be on the safe side I took live maggots as well, flavoured the same, to use on one rod as a comparison. Yes - I very nearly chickened out!

I was fortunate to get a mild and overcast October evening for my first attempt, so at least the fish would be feeding. They certainly were. I got eight tench, with two of them over 5lbs. Three came to the live maggots and FIVE to the dead ones. I was staggered. I had never before had eight tench in one evening at the pit, and it was only a three hour 30 minute session as well.

The bites to dead maggots had been supremely confident, with the indicator rising smoothly to the butt ring and staying there. I am sure the fish would have taken the rod in if I had let them, as each one was hooked well back in the mouth. I just had to go back again next evening, and even though it was much cooler, with a chill breeze, I got six more, four of them on deads again.

By now my mind was going like a washing machine on fast spin, and after hours of deliberation I decided to take a gamble. For the remainder of my time at the pit I would use dead maggots and no flake or caster added, and try several flavours. In the event I had barely three weeks before the onset of cold nights brought the feeding to a halt. During that time I caught several more tench and many small roach and perch, to half a dozen different flavour blends.

There could be no doubt about it, the dead maggots were a huge success, and I could see why when I dropped a couple of handfuls in the margins. They stopped exactly where I put them, very visible on the soft mud. I did further experiments, dropping a loaded feeder into shallow water. What happened was that the groundbait plugs slowly broke down, leaving two little piles of food, one at each end of the feeder. A few maggots rolled out, but the bulk of them only came out when the tackle was reeled in. The action of the suddenly moving feeder spewed the maggots over a distance of one to two feet. A sudden strike would leave a trail a yard or more long, as well as dispersing the groundbait over a similar area.

It was clearly necessary to make two or three rapid casts immediately I started fishing, to get some food in the swim, but no more than that. With this fishing not a single maggot is wasted, and I quickly realised that our ideas on correct feeding are based on live maggots, most of which disappear. The risk of over-feeding was obvious, and when bites were not coming quickly I started to make alternate casts with the feeder filled only with groundbait.

I could visualise the scene out there on the bottom, with maggots spread around among the accompanying streaks of groundbait, and the whole lot giving off the attractive aromas and tastes. A tench arrives and starts to vacuum the bottom, and the inert, almost weightless dead maggots are inhaled with no effort. The vortices created by the fins of the fish would cause both maggots and groundbait to lift from the bottom and eddy around, before slowly sinking again. This would attract other fish, which in turn would cause more disturbance. No wonder it worked...

This was great stuff. The problem of fishing on soft mud or silkweed had been well and truly solved, and good catches had been made. But these were fish which had never been subjected to pressure; fish I'd had all to myself. Also they had lost much of their natural food, and my offerings must have seemed like manna from heaven. What might happen when I tried it on the super-sophisticated denizens of the River Trent? Fish that have seen it all, and been subject to every level of angling competence, from ham-fisted novices to highly-skilled matchmen. Fish which are bombarded daily with feeders full of healthy, wriggling maggots of every type and size. I had to admit that I

The author (above) with his personal best pike, weighing 28lb. This one fell to conventional tactics - legered half mackerel - but during his experiments with flavoured maggots pike well into double figures have been caught in the dark! Could there be more impressive proof that fish respond to flavours? The picture below is also interesting, a 6lb 7oz river Trent carp and a 5lb chub which is almost the same shape. The author believes these short, fat chub are virtually a different species to the more normally shaped Trent chub. They are almost always caught in the dark, or in very highly coloured water during daylight. They are, in his experience, almost completely predatory, with sea fish chunks the best bait. This one was a rarity in that it fell to flavoured dead maggot, but all the other Trent species respond well to that bait.

had my doubts, but I also had hopes. The Trent may be swept clean from time to time by surging floods, but most of the time it has bottom sediment amply deep enough for maggots to hide in.

It had taken me some while to get used to handling these dead maggots. The initial feel was akin to handling cold custard which had formed a skin, and with no movement they stuck together in a soft mulch. Worse still they seemed to deteriorate very quickly once defrosted, and after about five hours they would steadily darken. For that reason I took them out of the freezer only a few minutes before going fishing. If they were still solid when I arrived at the water I could thaw a few hookbaits in seconds by just holding them between finger and thumb. They looked and felt so awful I began to feel quite sure that the Trent fish would turn up their noses at them, so I played safe by taking live maggots and one of my flavoured pastes.

It was a dull November afternoon when I arrived on the river, and still warm for the time of year. The river was low and stale after weeks without rain, and although I did not fancy my chances it was at least a change of scenery after the endless flogging away on the rudd pit. I set up my usual Trent quiver rod and hurled the feeder about a third of the way across. The bait was three dead maggots on a 14 hook to 4.6lb Ultima, and the maggots were flavoured with the Ultraspice, Sense Appeal and Protaste mix. The groundbait had been flavoured with the same, plus a teaspoon of Spice Appetite Stimulator. The water temperature was still above 60 degrees F., and I knew that a shoal of bream tended to hole up in the area in low water conditions. I hoped that I might contact them.

With the rod propped high in the rests I leaned back to watch a heron, standing motionless in the water against the far bank. I never cease to marvel at these birds; so huge and ungainly in flight, yet they can land on a fragile branch at the very top of a tree with all the grace of a ballet dancer. I once saw one flying low along the Trent, and it took a dead bleak from the surface with one neat and precise movement of its long neck. It was so fast it was almost a blur - like my quivertip suddenly was as it smashed towards the water. The butt came high off the ground with the tip actually touching the surface. I had to perform like a Division 1 goalkeeper to grab the butt and save the loss of the entire tackle. I found myself attached to a heavily running fish which simply surged downstream, making the clutch scream and giving me no chance to get the rod up. I could only hang on grimly, and luckily it finally turned and forged heavily back upstream. I gradually got it under control, and after a fight lasting about seven or eight minutes I netted a torpedo shaped common carp of exactly 10lbs.

I released it back into the river with trembling hands. Could this possibly be happening? It had been my first cast into the river with dead maggots, and within two minutes I was into a double figure carp! Making the second cast I sat with eyes glued to the quiver, all thoughts of bird life banished. Five minutes later, just when I was calming down, the tip went smoothly round. The heavy thud, thud on the rod told me it was a bream, and at 4lb 12oz it was a nice one. I did not really mind when the next cast produced a gudgeon, and as I fished on the tempo increased. A few roach put in an appearance, along with three perch, to be followed by a couple of good chub. Interspersed with these were skimmers, hybrids and the odd, good-sized bream. Most of the key Trent species had fallen already; dead maggots were not going to be dead ducks on this river after all. As the light started to fade my Betalight began to glow, and the better bream really got their heads down. Fish of 4lb, even 5lb, were coming regularly to the net, and I was now getting so many bites I began filling the feeder with groundbait only for two out of every three casts. It wasn't so much the fear of over-feeding; I was almost through my two pints of dead maggots and the need to economise was desperate. It wasn't until I got home that I remembered I had also taken live maggots as well!

I fished on into the dark for a couple of hours, and by then I had had enough. All through those two hours the bites had come within seconds of the feeder hitting bottom, and they all produced bream between 3lb 8oz and 5lb 4oz. I had long since stopped putting fish into the net for fear of over-crowding, but I still released in excess of 40lbs. Including the carp I suppose the total weight must have been over 100lbs. I slept the sleep of the dead that night; my overloaded brain was unable to take in any more.

At work next day, however, I could not stop thinking about it. All the species had picked up dead maggots without hesitation, and that carp had taken them without giving me any time to introduce any loose feed into the swim. I knew my flavour combinations were really pulling the fish in, but there had to be more to it than that. Surely it had to be that they were unafraid of dead maggots because they were totally different, and the fact that they were easily found helped to explain the rapidity of the bites.

Different they certainly were, for on the hook three maggots seemed to fuse together into an amorphous lump of unmentionable. But how they worked! With my flavours I am confident I can catch lots of fish on live maggots, but it would be physically impossible to catch any faster than I had with those dead baits. I also have the great advantage of instant bait, for as I write the freezer holds six pints, flavoured with six different blends, and all neatly labelled up. I can use them tomorrow or a year from now; they will be just as effective either way. Bad news for bait breeders, isn't it? There is no further need to waste maggots, or to see them deteriorate and turn to casters

Over the previous years I had had the privilege of making many terrific catches on the feeder, but what followed that November evening can only be described as the silly season. Big bags became the norm, anywhere I fished. I deliberately tried unfancied areas, swims I did not normally bother with, trying to make the approach fail; trying to find the flaws. The only real difference, though, was that I caught smaller fish from the poor swims, but just as many. It seemed as though they had lost all caution with flavoured and dead maggots. It was like turning the clock back 20 years, before the river became so pressurised, or waking up in Ireland or Denmark, where the fish still behave without hesitation or guile. Even in the cold water and high water levels of that winter the onslaught continued, slowing down only a little

I continued through what remained of the season, swapping around with the flavours, oils, aminos, sweeteners, all the combinations, finding those which worked best in given conditions, those which worked best for which species in given conditions, catching, catching, catching...

Then, right at the end of the season, it all turned a bit sour on me. I found that success had its problems. More and more the fish were swallowing the bait right down, and I was needing the disgorger almost every time. It all came to a head one March evening, when 12oz hybrids were yanking at the quivertip even before I could get the rod in the rests. Each one had swallowed the hook almost out of sight, and I hate the thought of damaging any fish. In desperation I pushed the no. 8 shot to less than two inches from the hook, but they just swallowed that as well. This was unbelievable, and as a last resort I changed the no. 8 for a BB, and set it just one inch from the hook. That virtually cured it, though even then some of the fish had the shot well inside their mouths when landed. The bites were so strong they were hooking themselves, and the only way to have a cup of coffee was not to cast out.

When the close season came around again it was time to sit back and take a long, hard look at things. I felt more strongly than ever that I had taken my feeder fishing as far as it could possibly go. Yes, there would be new baits, new additives to try, massive catches to be made, but for once I was not wishing away the next 12 or 13 weeks. I realised I did not want to begin the next season as I had finished the last, for I could see no real challenge in it. How could one improve on a fish every cast, practically every time out? I had to do something which was both different and harder.

At the time of writing I have had a year off feeder fishing, but I know I will return to it when a new target presents itself. I know a water which probably holds a record roach, and another which is said to hold large crucians. One or the other, or both, may be next on the list, but for the moment I am adapting some of what I have learned about the feeder to a new and certainly a much more difficult challenge - the capture of large carp from the River Trent. Everything I had learned about baits was applicable, I thought. So too were the tackle set-ups - my end of the tackle, anyway. I could see how the feeder itself could assist the process, and there were ideas in my head which were logical extensions of feeder fishing.

I had caught carp by accident, as it were, and seen quite big ones landed by friends. But could I succeed if I fished for them selectively? It was going to be fun to find out, but being me I had to have a target. I decided I would try and catch a Trent carp weighing more than 30lbs.

TRENT CARP

The more I thought about it the more it appealed to me - a Trent thirty! I didn't want a big gravel pit fish with a name like Humpy, Lumpy, Smiley, Scaley, Sally or whatever. Anglers could catch one of those in their very first season with bolt rigs and boilies, but somehow I could not see a beginner catching a river thirty. There was nobody around who could tell him what to do - a sobering fact I was soon to discover for myself.

I delved into the literature again, ready to absorb the knowledge as to how the carp experts tackled big rivers, and what their feelings and thoughts were about the many different problems posed by running water. And what did I find? Zilch! There are no river carp experts. There are a few people who have caught big river carp, yes, even thirties, but there isn't an angler who is catching 20lb plus river carp on a regular basis. On stillwaters there must be at least 50 such people, but on rivers the instant carper is totally lost, and many expert carpers are lost as well - suffering from the lack of all-round expertise they once thought they would never need. Once again I would have to learn for myself.

The one certain thing about lake and pit fishing is that Humpy, Lumpy or Sally is going to be there unless somebody has nicked them, but on a river that certainty is somewhat extended. Even if a fish is caught often enough to become known it could be anywhere between weirs, and might have gone over a weir in time of flood. That was the first thought which struck me; the enormity of the challenge I had set myself. The total volume of water in the Trent exceeds that of any stillwater many times over, and I felt certain the bigger fish would be long range travellers. In the 1970s I had done some research on the barbel of the Derbyshire Dove, and found that while the smaller fish occupied regular swims the larger ones travelled widely, turning up anywhere. In the 1980s I had pike-fished on the River Soar in Leicestershire and caught several fish which had been marked with blue dye, in a River Trent swim. Those particular fish had travelled 2.5 miles downstream and then gone a further half mile up the Soar, halting only because they then ran up against a large weir.

Yes, the large Trent carp would be travellers too, and I began to see what I was up against. Just what are the chances of turning up in a given swim at the same time as a 30lb carp, and finding it on the feed? And what bait would I need for such a fish? Fortunately I had a couple of friends who had been catching a few smaller carp, and they were using maize seeds. This seemed ideal to me. I knew it to be a very hard bait which would usually defeat the attentions of chub and bream, and I knew from experience that it would absorb flavoured water like a sponge. It would also be suitable for use in my big 'vacuum' feeders.

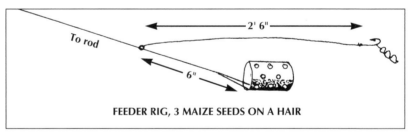

FEEDER RIG, 3 MAIZE SEEDS ON A HAIR

Fig. 28: Above the standard feeder rig, used with three maize seeds on a hair. Below the simple boilie/bolt rig. The lead has to be on a weaker link in case it snags up. Both rigs incorporate the small Drennan ring used in previously described feeder tackles.

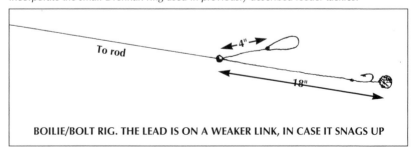

BOILIE/BOLT RIG. THE LEAD IS ON A WEAKER LINK, IN CASE IT SNAGS UP

On my second rod I elected to use ordinary bolt rig tactics, with a fixed lead and an Optonic to warn me of any takes. The two rigs looked like Fig 28 (previous page).

My first session was on a late August evening, with the river running low and clear, and at a temperature in excess of 70 degrees F. I carefully cast the bolt rig upstream and out of the way of my quiver rod, which I fished downstream in the more normal way. Both rods were baited with three maize seeds on a hair rig, flavoured with Scopex. I had not boiled the maize, but had soaked it for two days in the flavoured water. I feel that boiling can destroy some of the effectiveness of flavours, so simple soaking is better if you can get away with it.

I was soon getting all sorts of pulls and twitches on the quiver as the skimmers and hybrids did their best to get the baits off the hooks, and I cast regularly to get a layer of maize on the bed of the swim. A 12oz hybrid managed to get itself hooked, and was returned to its environment. I found myself enjoying a nice, sunny evening, but not for long! I was catapulting a load of seeds around the bolt rig when the Optonic exploded into life. No warning blips; just a sudden banshee scream that sent me nearly 3ft into the air. The rod was bucking wildly in the rests, and the line was disappearing from the free spool Baitrunner reel at an alarming rate. I picked up the rod, braced myself and put the reel into gear by turning the handle. The 1.75lb test carbon rod was immediately slammed into a tremendous curve, but it did not slow down the carp at all as it continued its downstream run. The speed and power was breathtaking, but suddenly it was gone.

The 10lb Dacron hook link had broken at the knot, and I cursed my "bad luck." It was, in fact, my first major mistake - wrong hook length material - but I will come back to that later. While I cussed I felt pleased at the same time, for it was, after all, an instant success. A carp had, at least, been persuaded to take a bait. I tackled up again and, half an hour later, the Optonic once more screamed into life, but it stopped after two or three seconds. Later I was to learn that chub regularly did this, taking a couple of yards of line in a rapid burst, but managing to avoid the hook. Trying to combat this I went through several versions of the hair rig before I settled on the rig I use now.

The incident wound me up, and as darkness fell I was hovering over the rod, willing the Optonic to go again. That almost cost me a set of tackle, for I heard the feeder rod crash off its rests into a pile of nettles. I got to it just in time, and after a short scrap had a 6lb common on the bank. After that only the skimmers showed an interest in the baits, but I went home on a big high. With a start like that I was clearly destined to become the greatest ever river carp angler, but that notion soon began to evaporate. The next three sessions were total blanks!

This really stopped me in my tracks, for time nowadays is an extremely precious commodity for me. I run a very busy office, and have to be available on the phone for the greater part of almost every working day. Financially it's great. If I need a new rod or two or three top of the range Shimano reels they are just a phone call away, but if I want to have 24 hours' carp fishing (a short session to most keen carp men) it is impossible. Five or six hours at once is as much as I can manage, with three or four hours more likely. Also this was 1989, in the final months of the rudd pit experience and the dead maggot discovery. It was all happening; I realised I could not commit myself completely to carp just yet.

Still, I changed my 10lb line to 12lb, and swapped the Dacron trace for 15lb Kryston Silkworm - reckoned by many to be the best soft hooklink material available. I do not share that opinion. On one of my blank sessions I broke this twice, quite easily, on bottom snags, and a third time by just casting out! The boilie and about six inches of hook length went soaring into the blue. Obviously a bad batch, but it seriously dented my confidence in such materials. By the next time I fished the Trent, in late September, I was using the latest state of the art multistrand. The piece I was using was rated at about 35lb BS, so that ought to do it. Some hope!

It was another lovely evening, as so many were that autumn, and again the bait was flavoured maize. As the light failed the Optonic screamed its message, and again I found myself attached to something which went on a truly awe-inspiring downstream run. Once again the line went slack. The 'super link' had parted three inches from the hook, and it looked suspiciously like a bite-off from the fish's throat teeth. Thoroughly downhearted I tackled up again, and half an hour later the same rod was off again. As I dived towards it, it suddenly stopped. I typical chub take, I thought, until I wound in and found the last three inches of the tackle bitten off again - and while the rod was still in the rests! This was crazy. There was clearly more to river carping than met the eye, but my main success had been to leave hooks in the mouths of carp. Not why I go fishing, so I dropped it and devoted all my attention to the dying days of the rudd pit.

It was late October before I tried again, and this time the hook link was the same as my main line, the ever-reliable 12lb Ultima nylon. I would defy modern carp fishing convention, so even my hair was made from 4.6lb Ultima. I also dropped the feeder but still adhered to the feeder principles by using PVA bags. To the uninitiated, PVA is a material that dissolves slowly in water, and the bags - available in many tackle shops - will hold far more maize seeds than even a very large feeder. I attach them simply by sticking the hook through the top of the bag and lobbing the lot into the swim. After a few minutes the bag dissolves, leaving a neat pile of seeds with the hair-rigged bait just on the edge of it. I then top up with several catapults full in the immediate area, the aim being to attract cruising fish by sending a flavour trail downstream. The strongest concentration of flavour is, of course, from that main pile of seeds beside the hook bait.

The carp evidently agreed with what I was doing, for just after dark the wailing Optonic signalled a take from a lively common weighing exactly 10lbs. Two evenings later I was back and had another common, this time 12lb 8oz. It fought very hard, but neither fish produced the blistering runs I had experienced previously. Obviously they were from much bigger fish, but how big? That question was beginning to haunt me...

Still, it was enjoyable catching carp which hooked themselves, a new experience for me. Once the set-up is right all you have to do is chuck two baits out and wait for the Optonic to sound. Then you play out a fish which is already hooked. No wonder so many young lads take up this form of fishing. Buy the latest tackle, half a ton of ready-made boilies, read for a few minutes and then sit it out at the local pit. Sooner or later a fish will take the bait, and you can then send your picture to the angling weeklies and show everyone how clever you are. In reality it can be the most boring fishing imaginable if the bites are not forthcoming, and I now faced a whole month of boredom.

I had been using different flavours on each of my two rods. One of the doubles had taken an oil flavour and the other had gone for fish. I never have and never will use the same attractor on both rods, as the tastes of the fish change more rapidly on the Trent than anywhere else. I theorise about the reasons why later on. Regular changes of flavour failed to produce results in the lean spell. The odd session after chub, barbel and pike saved me from complete boredom, but the mind remained fairly active. Besides swapping flavours I had also been trying several different swims, all with equal lack of success, so I knew something different had to be tried. Attention switched to the type of boilie to use - not your round, semolina-based mass-production baits but a real Archie Braddock special. It had occurred to me that all the biggest Trent carp that I had heard about in the past few years had been taken on plain bread flake, so my super-boilie would be based on bread crumb. Furthermore, it would be square, just because everyone else's were round.

Setting to work with a will, I mixed up many concoctions of crumb, soya, wheat gluten, rice, liver powder... you name it, I put a bit of it in. My early efforts were not a conspicuous success. Some just fell apart during the boiling process, others virtually melted, like PVA. Others cracked up as they dried out, and some would not go hard, even if they were boiled for 10 minutes. Eventually, however, I came up with a square, firm boilie which reeked of Clove spice E.A., so now I could go out and clean up. My turn to see my face, beaming in glorious technicolour from the pages of the weeklies...

It nearly worked! Towards the end of November a fresh start, in a new swim, produced a 9 p.m. take on my bread boilie. It did not feel very big and it came off half way to the bank, but it was only the first time out with the new bait. I gave a few to a friend, and in the same week he had a carp first time out, even if it was only 5lb 8oz. Was this it? No, I am afraid not. I had only one more take on the bait, another small fish of 7lbs, so I reluctantly abandoned it. Some of the thinking behind this bait was, however, to prove important later on.

One of my friends reported an 8lb common (all the carp seemed to be commons) on curry-flavoured maize, reminding me how well spicy flavours had worked for me with feeder maggots late in the season, so I made the switch to curried maize on one rod. It proved a wise move, for on my first December trip I had a common of 12lb 2oz, just after dark. With night falling at 5 p.m. all my fishing was being done in the dark anyway.

I had not yet given up on the boilies, but I clearly did not know enough about making them, so I went out and bought the best powder mix I could find - Rod Hutchinson's high protein. Five ml. of fish flavour, 5ml. of Shellfish Sense Appeal, six eggs and two minutes' boiling produced excellent boilies. How easy it is when the experts do it for you! Full of renewed confidence I arrived at the river on December 12, an evening which was to prove the turning point in my Trent carp fishing.

The river was still at summer level, due to the seemingly endless drought conditions, and it wasn't at all cold for December. The swim I had chosen was quite a snaggy area generally, culminating in one big underwater snag, probably an old tree, about 40 yards downstream. This was one of the few areas of the Trent to hold resident carp, thanks to those snags, but I was now confident of my tackle. I was also, now, casting mainly upstream, which caused the current flow to pull my Betalight indicator tight to the rod, so most bites would cause it to drop back quite rapidly as fish dislodged the lead (method described on page 64, Fig 23). For this reason I used very long front rod rests, with the rod pointing high in the air. It would enhance those drop-backs and keep as much line as possible out of the water. This has another great advantage when drifting weed or dead leaves are coming down in the flow, for all the flotsam collects in the bow of the line. It does not slide down to the lead, perhaps even masking the bait (See Fig. 29).

I started fishing with the fish-flavoured boilie upstream and the curry maize downstream, towards the snags. Just after dark I had two rapid drop-back bites on the boilies - the usual chub. I connected with neither, but at least the river was not dead. It was another hour and a half, though, before anything else happened. This time the indicator

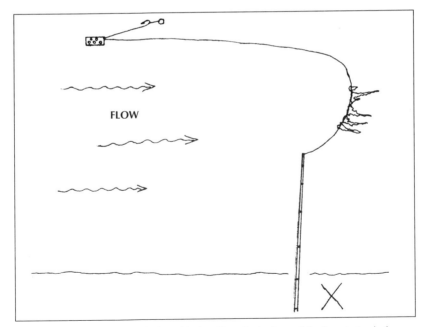

Fig. 29: Upstream legering. All the rubbish collects in the bow of the line, instead of sliding down to the lead and the hook, as it does when downstream fishing.

dropped back very slowly on the boilie rod, before rising back to the rod ring, at which point the Baitrunner purred into life.

The strike met with solid resistance, as they say, but this was no monthly magazine cliche. This was for real. The fish was powering upstream, and I knew instantly that I was into something special. I took it easy though, for the fish was heading away from known danger. After travelling perhaps 30 yards the carp just stopped, and hung there, totally ignoring the well-bent rod. Suddenly it was moving downstream, though, and I could sense that it was now alarmed. Its speed was building up, and as it came level with me I really crammed on the pressure, to no avail. The fish forged inexorably towards the snags.

The pressure on my arms was enormous, and the rod was bent to a ridiculous angle, but still the fish moved on. I had to stop it so I just clamped down hard and gave it everything I'd got; it was make or break. The 12ft carbon was now reduced to little more than 4ft of effective length, so far round was it pulled, and I waited with gritted teeth for the line, or maybe even the rod, to go with a crack. Neither thing happened. The fish had been stopped, but had suddenly woken up properly! Almost before I knew it the carp had screamed back upstream, passing me at unbelievable speed. All I could do was hang on to the straining rod and a buzzing reel, until suddenly it was gone! I wound in to find the nylon hook link severed as neatly as if done by scissors. When a fish is travelling at that speed on a very taut line it has only to brush against a rock, an old tin can or whatever, and the effect is the same as using a guillotine.

I sank into my chair almost stupified by the power of the fish. If I'd had the time I might have remembered that the biggest Trent carp I knew about had been landed with no trouble at all, in five or ten minutes. I might have wondered which of my angling implements was the most reliable suicide weapon, but I did not have the time. The moment my trembling body hit the chair the other Optonic burst into life! I floundered through the mud and made a hasty strike. I hit nothing, and stood there gaping stupidly, brain not functioning at all. It took a full two seconds to realise that the clutch was still whizzing away and line hissing through the rod rings. I'd struck with the Baitrunner in free spool mode, and the fish was still on there, taking line. Panicking now, I completely forgot that the anti-reverse was engaged. I thumbed the lever forward to engage the clutch, which had been set pretty tight in consideration of those snags. The effect was spectacular, to say the least. The rod was slammed down to water level and the line broke with a devastating crack!

I will not attempt to convey my feelings. It took me a full half hour to recover and tackle up the two rods in order to start fishing again, and all the time I was pondering one inescapable fact. The bigger Trent carp had, so far, made a complete prat of Archie Braddock. When the maize rod eventually went again I was prepared for mighty battle, but it proved to be an easily subdued 10lb 13oz common. What an evening; all four and a half hours of it. Walking back to the car I re-lived my misfortunes and blundering incompetence, and resolved that next time it was going to be different.

Next time was a long time coming. The Trent, marvellous river though it is, can throw some real wobblers, and this time it came up with a big one. Before I could return the longest drought since 1976 ended, with the heavens opening. The river rose six feet overnight, and a howling wind stripped dead leaves from the trees by the ton. I had hooked those two monsters in mid-river, but for the rest of the season was unable to hold bottom there, with rotting leaves and other rubbish continually coming down an almost permanently high and dirty river.

I just fished for chub and pike, and anything else which might feed in those conditions. Whenever the level dropped a bit I fished for the carp if I could find a swim out of the heavy flows. I found some fish in the bankside slacks, all commons, but the best of them barely made 10lb.

Bites on maize had dried up altogether, with only the boilies producing takes. I had never thrown more than a dozen free offerings, but now I restricted this even more, using a four bait stringer only. A stringer is made up from the previously mentioned soluble PVA in string form, with the boilies threaded on with a needle. A knot is tied to stop the baits sliding off, and the other end of the string is tied to the bend of the hook. When cast out the PVA dissolves, leaving a line of baits immediatelty behind the hookbaits - exactly the same principle as the feeder (see Fig 30, next page).

During my semi lay-off that winter I gave a lot of thought to my approach, which had clearly been found wanting. Bite registration may sound like the least of my worries, but it was a problem to solve. Chub have a great liking for the boilies, and on good nights I was getting all sorts of odd bleeps from the Optonics. Some were from drifting rubbish, obviously, but I needed to know every time I had a chub bite. They signalled the fact that my stringer baits had all gone; obviously a chub would not take the tethered bait until all the free samples were

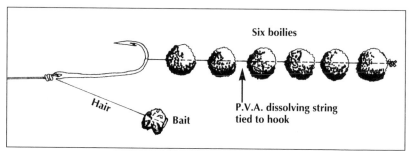

Fig. 30: The standard stringer rig. The boilies are strung out on dissolving PVA string, which is tied to the bend of the hook. The hair rig is tied to the eye of the hook, and the bait becomes the seventh in line for a carp working its way upstream.

eaten. After some thought I swapped my ordinary tip rings for threaded rings, enabling me to screw in a Betalight fitting, which I made myself (See Fig. 31). With my end tackles basically fixed paternosters (as shown in Fig. 28), plus the weighted Betalight bobbins at the butt ring, I would now be able to see every twitch, tap or pull. Everything I have since learned has confirmed that this basic approach is correct. As in feeder fishing it is essential that the loose feed is close to the baited hook, and it is just as essential to know when that loose feed has been cleaned up, and needs replacing.

Feeding rates

All good anglers, and particularly the best matchmen, know just how important the correct rate of feed is, but I doubt if one carp angler in 20 gives it any thought at all. The best ones will observe the movements of fish, make an educated guess as to how many fish are likely to be in the swim, and feed boilies or particles (seeds) accordingly. The vast majority just rush to their favourite swims, fill them in with 200 to 300 boilies and then sit back with a bait in the middle of it all, for days on end. Sooner or later they get a good fish, and proclaim to the angling world that they have the right method, 'cos look what I've caught...'

Of course, quite often, this approach has worked on the Trent, and the lucky angler has caught half a dozen fish in a session, with maybe a 20 among them. But this is often only luck, and the catch is unrepeatable. The angler had simply dropped on a group of fish which were in the swim at the time. Next day they could be a couple of miles away. If it is an area which regularly holds carp the swim gets

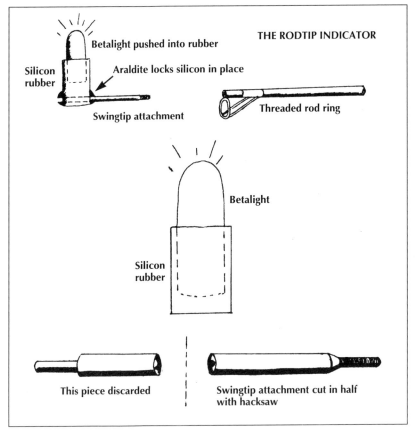

Fig. 31: The various components of the screw-in Betalight, and how they all fit together.

hammered and ultimately the fish move out, with the biggest ones leaving first.

My years on the Trent (is it really 40?) have left me in no doubt that the majority of big fish are travellers, and carp are no exception. Unless I am fishing a known hotspot I always assume there are no carp there when I arrive. Hopefully one or two will move through in the 2 to 4 hours I will usually spend there. Yes, I often fish for just two hours, but feel at no disadvantage. Why fish a 10 hour session when the carp feed for only two hours? Why not fish five times for two hours...? It's all about getting to know the feeding spells. To return to the main point, however, if a carp comes through my swim during my short session I do not want to confuse it with different flavour trails from all over the river. The sole attraction must be within inches of my hook-bait, and, of course, it is. The only departure I make from this approach is when I combine particle and boilie fishing. In this case I flavour both boilies and maize with, say, Ultraspice, and fish the boilie with a mere two bait stringer in the middle of a carpet of maize.

I say carpet, but perhaps you could call it a scatter, as I put it in with a catapult, not attempting to spread it right across the river. The second rod is baited with the maize itself, and fished close by. The theory is basically the same; there is a wider flavour trail, but still the centre of attraction is my hook-bait. If a carp starts hoovering up the particles only the second rod covers that eventuality. No, this approach does not overfeed the carp, as bream and chub will take care of quite a large proportion of the maize. With so few boilies out there the chances of a carp picking up mine are greatly multiplied, and of course my sensitive rig, described earlier, tells me instantly if nuisance fish are pulling at the bait. If so the stringer is quickly replaced.

On rare occasions there is clear evidence that several carp are in the swim. They may start to crash out of the water in the baited area, which calls for a response. I still don't throw in any loose feed but I do put out two seven bait stringers (one tied to the lead) and make perhaps three casts in 20 minutes. This can be repeated regularly, and it does not take a mathematical genius to work out how many boilies can be put into the swim within one hour - all of them where you want them to be.

I saw a classic example of how not to do it recently. I had set up in an area known to produce carp fairly often, and was tackling it as described above. Shortly after I had set up an angler I knew slightly arrived on the opposite bank, and gave me a cheery wave. He put his kit down and proceeded to catapult boilies all over the river, stopping after about 200 to tackle up. He then cast out and fired another 100 around his baited hooks. Half way through the evening session he blasted yet more in, many of them going way past mid-river into my swim. Neither of us had a bite, for obvious reasons, but at least I had not wasted a lot of money. I take with me about 50 boilies per rod, and most times half of them go back home to be frozen up and used again.

A lot of this had still to be discovered in that first long and wet winter, but I had instinctively set out on the right track, thanks to the feeder fishing experience. As that season drew towards its close I despaired of ever finding a fishable level, but at last, seven days before the close, I arrived at a new swim, to find the level at its lowest for two months. It was still up and dirty, but I could fish at about five yards range in 12ft of water, so I settled for that. I used my fish flavoured boilie on one rod while opting for sardine chunk on the other, with chub in mind. And it happened again!

Just after full dark the boilie rod roared off, and this time I did nothing wrong. With a correctly set clutch, and well in control of myself, I planted my feet wide apart and leaned into the fish. I might just as well have tried to stop a double decker bus. Treating my 12lb line like 2lb that carp set off on a downstream run which just went on and on. Then came the familier blip, and the line went slack. Once more I found the hook length sheared off, as if by razor blade. Obviously the fish had run into an unknown obstacle - unknown to me, anyway. I suspect the fish knew it well enough.

I nearly threw my tackle into the river in sheer frustration. What the asterisking hell had I got to do to land one of these things? Even the subsequent capture of a 4lb 3oz chub on the sardine rod did not mollify me. When I finally calmed down I resolved to come back the following evening, so I chucked in my remaining boilies - about 40 of them. A year on I would consider that a big mistake, though it seemed a good idea at the time. That following evening I had four takes on the fish boilie and caught four common carp, the biggest 8lb, the smallest 4lb, plus another chub of 4lb 3oz on the sardine. I went home quite pleased, not realising that I had reduced my chances of a big fish by drawing so many small ones into the swim.

Incidentally, it was not faulty line which was losing me those big fish. I was using a Trilene XL nylon hook link of 12.2lb BS on this latest occasion, and it had been cut off as easily as the Ultima before it.

More rain spoiled the last few days and it was March 14, the last day, before I got my next chance. On that occasion I fished from 5.30 to 11.15 p.m., a long time, by my standards. The river looked dead, the sky was clear and a very cold wind was blowing. My boilie was taken twice, at 8.15 by an 11lb 8oz common and at 11 p.m. by another of 8lb 12oz. In spite of catching two carp in a short time I found it all slightly boring, with nothing happening, but for those brief bursts of action, over the whole six hours. That's always been my problem. Once I have made something work I am impatient to move on to the next stage.

It still left me with a lot to think about during the close season. If we did not have one I would never get any serious thinking done! I had contacted 25 carp, some of them very big, in a fairly short period, considering the enforced lay-off with the weather, but I had landed only 15 of them, and none of the big ones. I must have been doing something right, and I certainly had a good bait in the fish boilie, but I did not know what to make of those lost fish. Ask yourself. If you had experienced what I had been through, what would your next move be!

At least I could sort out the boilie making in the next 13 weeks, as I did not want to keep using someone else's creation, no matter how good. (For once I agree with the wife. I am an awkward so and so). So, once more into the literature I went to read up on the composition of boilies, and by the time the next season came around I was producing very good boilies of my own. Perhaps that is a good cue to cover in more detail every carp angler's favourite topic - bait.

Boilies

If you are looking for a new and foolproof recipe you are not going to find one here. What I hope to explain is a principle, the principle I fish to. Basically I consider the carp population to be regular travellers, with the biggest fish the ones which travel the furthest. I try to attract any fish going through my swim into taking my bait, and I have already explained a little of that. It follows that the bait should be as good as you can make it, but that does not necessarily mean loads of expensive high protein milk powder.

The first requirement is a dense, heavy boilie; one that will sink rapidly and stay put on the bottom, not drift away out of the swim with the current. The best ingredient for this is semolina, which also happens to be very cheap, and easily available. Soya flour is another good, cheap ingredient, and I buy it as Soyolk, which I have mentioned previously. These two ingredients constitute 80% of my basic boilie mix in the summer. As the carp have shown a great liking for maize I always have some maize gluten in the mix. This is a powdered product derived from ground maize, and is available from carp bait firms and many of the larger tackle shops, as indeed are most of the items mentioned here. On page 52 I described vitamin supplements, and a percentage of that goes in the mix as well. Rice is another solid, heavy item, so I bung a bit of that in. I always have an appetite stimulator, mostly one which matches the flavour I am using, and that constitutes the basic mix I use regularly on the Trent, with the exception of one item the keen carp man would never dream of using - bread crumb. I have some of this in all my mixes, no matter what the flavour, and for a very important reason. I am fishing very short sessions and I want to get the fastest possible flavour leak-off from my boilies. The bread crumb gives the mix a sort of open weave texture, which is very important, as I will shortly explain.

I make up a lot of base mix in the close season and store it in airtight tins, ready for use. A rough breakdown of 1lb of this mix would be:

8oz Semolina
4oz Soyolk
1oz bread crumb
1oz Maize Gluten
1oz Vitamin Supplement
1oz Rice
1 heaped teaspoon Appetite Stimulator

Before making boilies I weigh out about 15oz of the base mix and add 1oz of Whey protein powder to it. This is a very fine milk powder, high in protein, but more important it has excellent binding qualities and helps to hold the mix together. That's mainly why I use it. It is sold as Gelpro by S.B.S. Baits, and by other names by other companies.

I then take four size 2 eggs, add 5ml of my chosen flavour, and beat them together. All that remains then is to add the powder mix to the eggs/flavour, and continue mixing until I have a good, firm paste. If the result is a bit too soft I just add more base mix until it comes right. Nothing revolutionary about that, as every good carp man would tell you, but from there I do it different. I roll the dough into long sausage like strips (by hand) and then chop it into chunks with a knife. These chunks become my boilies, and their size is governed by how thick one rolls the sausages. To complete the process I drop my baits into boiling water, about half a dozen at a time, for about 60 seconds, and leave them to dry for about six hours. This produces a good, firm boilie which is still a bit soft in the centre.

The finished product is a Shredded Wheat shaped bait, very porous at both ends where I cut the sausage strips. That's the result of using bread crumb. These open weave ends let the flavour out much faster, and when a carp tests a bait with its barbels it comes into direct contact with the ingredients - the vitamin powder or the maize gluten, for example. I do not think that happens with the ordinary marble-shaped boilie, as the eggs seal in all the ingredients and a lot of the flavour. Yes, I know carp fanatics will be screaming that my boilie will let in water, which ruins the bait, but I am only fishing for a few hours. I find it no trouble at all to replace a bait now and again. Also, for those who think higher protein levels are necessary, up to 50% of the base mix can be replaced by Casein 30 Mesh without ruining the bait.

So there you have my basic approach, dictated by the availability of my time - fast leak-off boilie (Ethyl-alcohol flavours are ideal), limited numbers of free baits close to the hook via stringers, and sensitive bite detection methods to ensure my stringers are topped up at the right time. I fish for perhaps nine to twelve hours a week in three or four evening sessions - not as much as the average carp fan puts in on one overnight stay - but it is enough. Most of the time I put in covers a major feeding spell, up to and after dark. All fish will feed then, if the conditions are suitable, but that brings us into the realms of the unknown and the little known, as far as the Trent is concerned.

All the time I have battled to master the Trent with special baits I have noted things which have been hard to explain - why a particular bait would work one day and maybe not the next, in seemingly identical conditions. Some of the reasons I identified and have explained, but others baffled me. I began to suspect that pollution - whatever was in the water at any given time - had a direct bearing on the effectiveness of baits.

When you are into special baits you are into chemistry, whether you like it or not. Chemical reactions are impossible to predict unless you know everything in the equation. How were my chemicals reacting with the chemicals and metals which form part of the legal and illegal discharges into the Trent? When there was no adverse reaction were they working? When there was an adverse reaction caused by Factor XYZ is that why I did not catch?

This is a subject which could become vastly more complicated than I promised you I would get, but I do now believe that the ever-changing content of the Trent helps to explain why we need plenty of alternative bait flavours. Those who fish waters which are more stable are very lucky, for when they find a bait which works the chances are they can keep it going for quite a long time. The Trent, however, is a constantly changing environment, even before they let the pollution get out of hand, especially in the area below Nottingham. The levels are constantly changing, as are the temperatures, especially at weekends. The quality of the water fluctuates too, from clear to muddy, and if my suspicions are right the pollution is greater on some days than on others, and probably also differs according to the time of day (or night).

Put yourself in the place of the polluter. If you want to let something really nasty go when would you do it? Correct. At night, when nobody is likely to see it. I have often seen foam appear on the river late at night, which leads me to believe the quality of the river often drops after midnight. That may be the reason for a phenomenon which is otherwise hard to explain - why there is a marked feeding spell from mid to late morning. Fellow carpers have discovered that while they turn up at dawn they usually catch nothing until about 10 a.m., and that nearly all their fish come between 10 and 12 noon. A dawn feeding spell would be more logical - but not if the river is still in its "morning after the night before" mode. A drop in quality overnight would slowly correct itself the following morning, setting the stage for a late morning feeding spell. Right or wrong, there is no arguing that the late morning feeding spell is a fact, and it is one I cannot usually take advantage of myself.

Creating a bait which will work in all the conditions to be expected on the Trent is clearly difficult to impossible, and here I must explain that I am talking about the Trent above Trent Bridge. Virtually all the Trent fishing I have covered in this book has been done in the part of the Trent which, according to the NRA experts, is now better than it has ever been since the industrial revolution. Good as it is said to be - and good as we know it to be - the river is still about 50 per cent treated sewage, don't forget. I am talking about the effects of metals, chemicals and mini pollutions in the good part of the river. Quite what we now do in the bad part, below Nottingham, is anyone's guess.

I can theorise, however. Towards the end of 1991 we began to hear a lot about the problems emanating from the sewage outfall at Stoke Bardolph. The biggest problem is ammonia, which is said to be going in, at times, at a lethal dose per litre of water. What is the most commonly used bait? Maggots, of course. And what do maggots produce? Ammonia! What is the least sensible bait to offer fish in such circumstances? Maggots?

It is certainly hard to justify the use of untreated maggots, and the case for giving them a different smell - which I established to my own satisfaction quite some time before ammonia was identified as a problem - is now surely ironclad. Anglers would be mad not to do it, but what are the lessons for carp enthusiasts?

In the short-term I suspect that the best way to avoid adverse chemical reactions is to stop using chemical flavours in baits. It is early days yet, but I am already a little way towards proving that natural substances, oils like Geranium, for example, are more effective on the Trent than chemical flavours such as Strawberry. They are currently out-scoring chemical baits by 6 to 1, but despite the reservations I have expressed I am reluctant to abandon chemicals altogether. My instincts tell me there ought to be a chemical flavour, or combination of flavours, which overcomes the ammonia or even neutralises its effect. Who knows, maybe a flavour exists which can react *favourably* with ammonia, and actually make a bait more attractive. Now however, I have jumped ahead of myself. Back into the Tardis for the short journey back to 1990.

1990

I started my first full carp season for more than 20 years with an all night session, or more precisely just five hours from midnight on June 15th to around 5 a.m. One rod was baited with the previous season's winning fish boilie, and the other with an untried sweet boilie. For the first hour I had regular chub pulls on both baits, and was kept busy replacing stringers. Finally it all quietened down, and I had at least half an hour of total silence.

Them without any warning, the sweet bait was away, the Optonic bleeping unusually slowly. When I lifted into the fish it carried on downstream at the same slow pace, completely ignoring my heavy pressure. Realising that once again I was connected to something special I eased off, and the fish immediately stopped, then started to come back upstream at an equally sedate pace. As it came level with me the hook pulled out! I screamed aloud in the dark. "Oh, no!" Not two hours into the season, and I had already lost yet another big fish. I did not know whether to cry or tear my hair out.

Nothing else happened through the night, and it was a very disgruntled angler who went home an hour after dawn, wishing he had a gun to shoot the flaming birds. I mean, why should they sing so happily while I felt so miserable? Worse still, I did not touch another carp for the next six trips, despite trying regular changes of boilies, plus reverting to the flavoured maize again. I caught a succession of chub up to 3lb 8oz on all the baits. Then, on June 30th, I had a 14lb 8oz common on three maize seeds, flavoured with Chocolate Malt. My fish boilie had done nothing at all, so I gave the recipe to a mate for him to try. He promptly caught a 16lb common the first time out, but it proved a false alarm. The bait did not catch another carp throughout the summer and autumn. Even in winter it never lived up to my expectations, which were, of course, based on the previous winter's results. I repeat ... there is no winning flavour combination on the Trent; only a constant struggle to stay in touch with the ever-changing preferences of the fish.

During July I started to catch carp from a number of swims on a variety of baits, but all of them were commons from around 12lbs down to as low as 5 or 6lbs. Flavoured maize was as good a bait as any, but I used a different flavour almost every time out, in the search for that one big fish. The odd carp I saw taken by other anglers was in the same size range, and it bothered me. I decided to do some ageing of the fish by reading their scales, something the Fisheries Office at the old Severn-Trent Water Authority had taught me how to do years ago. The results gave me something of a shock.

The Trent is *not* full of young, vigorously growing fish, all ultimately destined to make 20lb plus. The vast majority of the carp population averages a mere 1lb a year weight increase, and when you consider their growing span covers about 15 years then it is obvious they are never going to make big fish. It is equally obvious, however, that a small percentage do go through to become twenties and over. The chances of arriving in a swim at the same time as one of the really large fish began to look even slimmer. Who knows, maybe I had already used up all my chances.

I could only soldier on, and this I did, taking the odd small common, but it gradually began to emerge that one of my baits was starting to produce takes regularly. It was a boilie based on bird foods, incorporating ingredients like Robin Red, P.T.X., Nectarblend and Red Factor. All these powders can be obtained from the specialist carp suppliers and none of them are new, as they have been used since the 1970s. All I did was mix an ounce of each together, and add the same amount of my semolina/soya mix, previously described. To this was added 5ml of a spicy flavour, the usual four size 2 eggs, following by the rolling, chopping and boiling.

As August came in the river level dropped steadily in near drought conditions, and the water temperature regularly ran into the high 70s F. On one occasion it reached a staggering 83 degrees F. In these conditions my bird food boilie outfished everything else. Chub became almost a plague, and even 1lb to 2lb bream started hooking themselves on. I had to put up with it, for among all the nuisance fish came a steady trickle of carp, albeit all small commons. Bites on other baits virtually dried up, probably due to the blistering conditions. Suddenly there came a short break in the heatwave, with a couple of days of blustery weather bringing heavy skies and occasional sharp showers.

I deliberately picked a swim with the wind in my face to get the maximum benefit from its water cooling effects. I started fishing at 6.30 p.m., but all was quiet until 8.30 p.m. when my birdfood rod blasted off. I found myself attached to a lively carp which rolled and showed itself to be in the 15/16lb bracket. And suddenly, yet again, it was gone! The line had broken at the knot, and there is no excuse for that. It is angler failure. In my misery I almost turned to prayer. Please God don't let this be happening to me; I'll be good and go to church every Sunday... The only answer I got was a sudden shower, which soaked me.

I tackled up and cast in again, then slumped dejectedly into the chair. At 9.10 p.m. the same rod screamed off again, and once more I found myself fighting a lively fish. After two or three minutes I had the carp, a common of about 10lb, on its side and sliding towards the net. The hook pulled out! I stood still for a full minute, then looked round for a gun to shoot myself with.

But that incredible evening was not yet over. I can scarcely remember tackling up again, but can recall sitting in the chair working out which method of suicide was the least painful. I was still pondering that problem when the same rod was away again. This time the Optonic ticked away quite slowly, and I leaned into the fish almost casually. After all, I was going to lose it, wasn't I? The carp moved away upstream, deep, slow, powerful. At that moment the wind suddenly increased, the already darkening sky got blacker and rain scythed across the river, straight into my face. I could not hold back a cynical laugh. What more fitting conditions could there be to lose another fish in?

The wind, blowing against the straining line, created an eerie whining noise, much as it does when it whistles around an old house, late at night. Five minutes later I became aware of two things; the fish was still on, and it was BIG! At ten minutes my arms were aching, my heart was pounding, my knees were shaking and the fish was tiring. Was I really going to land it? At 12 minutes it rolled into the net, its final tail lash sending muddy water all over my already soaked figure. It was the season's first mirror carp, all 24lbs 10oz of it. The fish was suffused in a rosy glow that you only seem to get from Trent fish, and when I lifted it the belly was just as firm as the back. It was a solid,

"It was the first mirror of the season, at 24lb 10oz..."

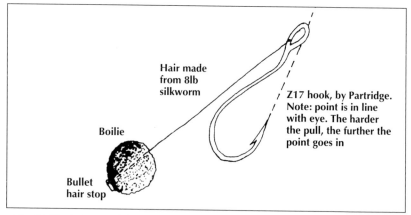

Fig. 32: The hair-rig and the crucial hook type. Note also the length of the hair.
Wherever the bait falls, in relation to the hook, a fish can take it without feeling metal.

muscular chunk of a fish, quite unlike so many of the dropsy-gutted biggies from stillwaters. It is no wonder they fight so hard.

I scarcely remember going home that evening, just three and a half hours after I first cast in, but two days later I was back again. I got bites from start to finish on my bird food bait, a series of chub from 2lb 8oz to 4lb 3oz and three small commons between 8lb 8oz and 9lb 8oz, all in four hours. My diary entry for that date, August 17th, reads: "I have a winner of a bait."

High as I was I still thought about that fish which came off the hook, and other odd ones that had done the same, so I spent a lot of time messing about with different lengths and positions of the hair. I finally arrived at the rig I now use permanently, and which is basically a return to the original principle of the hair rig. The hair, made from 8lb Silkworm, is tied from the eye of the hook, and is made long enough so that however it lies in relation to the hook a fish can always pick it up without feeling metal (See Fig. 32). Although I had caught all my carp so far on nylon hook links I felt it was time to try soft links again, and the new Kryston Super Silk fitted the bill perfectly. It is rated at 14lb breaking strain, but in fact, after being knotted and soaked for hours, it still breaks above 14lbs. It was this material I was using when I pulled that double mattress upstream against a winter flow, as mentioned in a previous chapter.

I was still walking on air on August 25 when, instead of fishing, I took my wife for a walk down the river. (I know, don't tell me. I spoil her). During that nice summer's evening I came across an angler I will call Mike, as he is not one to chase publicity. He was standing in the river with his large landing net in the water, and was in a state of great agitation. When he saw it was me, and not some inquiring stranger, the dam broke.

"I've got a huge carp, probably 29lbs," he gasped, and with that he lifted the net to display the biggest and certainly the longest common carp I had ever seen. Huge as it was I just felt it wasn't quite that heavy, and I immediately despatched the wife the mile and a half home to fetch my scales, weigh sling and camera. (Well, she did say she fancied a walk!). On her return I ascertained the weight as 27lb 6oz, a belter of a fish. Once again it was solid in the belly and immensely thick across the shoulders. I was really pleased for Mike, who had fished for Trent carp a lot longer than I had, and deserved his success. Nevertheless, I could not help feeling a tiny twinge of jealousy.

Still, there was concrete proof that big fish inhabited that area, so I left the downstream section, where I had taken my 25, and concentrated on this upstream water. My catch rate immediately dropped, as it became obvious that far fewer carp were around in this section of river. Indeed, the first four sessions were complete blanks, despite my killer bait.

The monster

On September 5 I tried once more, to find the river totally dead. I fished a long time by my standards, from 6.30 to 10.50 p.m., and then started to pack away. At exactly 11 p.m. I reached for my remaining rod, baited with the bird food boilie, and the Optonic burst into hesitant life. Marvelling at this last minute chance, and realising that these slower bites often heralded bigger fish, I checked everything before leaning into the carp. It took off heavily downstream, and I was content to let it go. I had hooked it just below a small bush, and it was fully 150 yards downstream to the next known obstacle, a big willow, so I had plenty of room to play the fish in. On top of that I was using a much more powerful carbon rod I usually reserved for piking, coupled with Ultima 12lb line and the new Super Silk trace. After that sodden mattress incident I was supremely confident in the tackle.

I suddenly realised that the fish had covered more than half the distance to the big willow, so I grabbed the landing net in one hand and set off after it. After a 100 yard stumble through the nettles and thistles I paused to take up the slack. There wasn't any. The fish had easily matched my pace and was still cruising unstoppably downstream. Something had to be done, so I buried the rod butt in my waistline and leaned back hard. It went into an undreamed of curve

"It gave me the chance to photograph a lovely common of 14lbs, with a background of snow..." (see page 134).

and, quite against my will, I found myself staggering downstream that last 50 yards. The pace and direction of the fish did not change at all; it was as if I wasn't there.

Butterflies started to flutter in the pit of my stomach. What was I attached to? I now came up to the willow, beyond which I could not go, but the fish could - and did. I stood there, helplessly, the tip of the rod round level with the reel. The clutch was ticking remorselessly and the muscles in my arms and back were crying out in protest. What next? I wondered. The carp fishing equivalent of being keelhauled? This monster felt like it could drag me through that big willow, but instead it stopped - probably of its own accord. The bend slowly went out of the rod, and it took me a few seconds to realise that the fish was coming back upstream, which might give me a chance to get in control. I had not been, thus far! Pumping steadily I waited until I guessed the carp to be directly opposite me, and then crammed on pressure to the limit. I intended to force the carp off its chosen line; to swing it in nearer my bank. Not a chance. It carried on upstream with the same dogged and immense power, and I had no choice but once more to go stumbling after it. This was crazy; I felt I had more chance of breaking my leg than of landing that fish. It was absurd and dangerous to be dashing around in the dark.

About half way up the straight the fish stopped again, and I stopped with it, thankful for the rest. The rod was well bent, with the tip nodding slowly as the great fish just hung out there in the current. I sneaked a look at my watch - 11.12 p.m. Assuming that the fish would be tiring I made a bad mistake, cramming on the pressure again. It responded by forging off upstream once more, but this time slightly faster and just as unstoppable. I finished up back at the spot where I had hooked it, by the little bush, but the fish continued its upstream surge, still absolutely impervious to everything I did. That wasn't much. I just stood there with the rod doubled over, listening to the clutch purring its deadly message - that my line was steadily disappearing from the spool. Miracle of miracles, it stopped again. The rod slackened and once more the fish came downstream, passing me and carrying on. Before I knew it I was back against the big willow. The fish had now taken me for a 450-yard walk in the dark, and the line was still disappearing.

From here the memory is hazy, but I do remember above all the screaming agony in my arm muscles from the prolonged and intense strain. The carp made that up and down journey at least once more; it had now walked me almost half a mile! The next clear memory is of standing half way down the straight, the fish sulking menacingly and unmovingly in mid-river. I was almost sobbing with relief as the pressure temporarily relaxed. I took another chance to glance at the watch - 11.30 p.m.

Suddenly and quite unexpectedly the fish surfaced. Even in the dark I could see the huge swirl. Could it possibly be tiring? Tentatively, this time, I increased pressure again and felt the fish swing ponderously and oh so grudgingly towards me. Scarcely daring to breath I kept the pressure as smooth as I could and in she came, a vast, sullen weight. Ten yards from the bank the carp broke surface again with another tremendous swirl, before forging powerfully down deep and away once more. Definitely tiring, but not finished yet!

This time I back-wound against her, gradually increasing pressure by slowing down the back-wind. It worked. The fish slowed and slowed, until it came to a stop. I held the rod well bent as I waited for its head to swing round towards the bank. The rod stayed like that, bent right over, and everything went deathly still. The line was snagged solid on an obstruction I did not even know existed. It was 11.35 p.m., and 10 minutes later I broke the line with a straight pull, after trying everything I knew to get it free. I do not have to describe how I felt. Every angler who reads this will understand. That event will stay with me forever, like a scar. Maybe I should have gone to church, like I promised.

At least I had a fantastic bait, and during the rest of September I caught three more carp on it, all small commons again. And that was it! Not another take did I get on it that season, and I automatically assumed it was a summer only, high water temperature bait. The following season I went straight in with it, but not another run have I ever had on it, summer or winter. Like I said, the Trent can throw you some real wobblers, and that was a big one.

I still had lots of flavours to try on the maize, which I did, and a freezer full of different boilies I had made in the close season, so I still managed to pick up the odd small common as the 1990 season went on. While I was trying out my baits I witnessed another big fish capture on September 18th. Mike caught the big common again, this time at 28lbs, on the same bait in the same swim. I could not help feeling a bit choked, for he had now caught it twice while I had been there, and I had come nowhere near it. For the record it fought hard, and was landed in 13 minutes on 11lb line. How big is a carp which will not be beaten in 35 minutes on 12lb line?

On October 7 I tried a new area altogether with a new boilie flavour, and came up with a mirror of just under 18lbs, first time out. Naturally I returned to the spot, and had five consecutive blanks, proving that the fish had just been travelling through. From then on the wobbler factor came with a vengeance. Throughout the rest of October, November, December and January I struggled. I tried many different areas, and all the different baits, and I did catch a few carp. All of them were commons from as small as 3lb and up to 13lb. By any definition these were stunted fish, for a carp which reaches its maximum growth at about 14lbs can only be described thus.

What really defeated me was the weather. As I discussed earlier, the conditions change extremely rapidly on the Trent, and even though I checked the river nearly every day it still caught me out several times. What can you do with a water that is perfect at 1 p.m. yet 18" up and thick with mud when one arrives at 6 p.m.?

What I did, in fact, was to fish for chub on one rod, with the sardine chunks. Chub will feed in high, coloured water, but not carp, and unless you can find a backwater it is a waste of time fishing for them. The chub fishing, though, was excellent, with many fish over 4lbs coming my way. The second rod produced the occasional small carp on boilies - just enough to keep the pot boiling. I did briefly return to feeder fishing, digging out my big vacuum feeders. I used groundbait plugs flavoured the same way as my boilies, and used 6 or 7 boilies in the feeder. I did not continue with it for very long, for it did not feel right. To make the flavoured groundbait work means re-casting every two or three minutes, otherwise the bream and chub rapidly clear it up. I did not think that would give me much chance with cruising carp, with the tackle out of the water so much of the time. In any case, stringer fishing is just a slowed down version of feeder fishing, without the groundbait.

On December 8 we had the biggest snowfall for many years, with half the country blocked. Ten days later, with the river within its banks after the snow had thawed, I had a good session. Fishing tight to the bank to avoid the rubbish coming down with the current I had carp of 9.8, 11.12 and 12.8, plus chub of 3.0 and 3.14. Not bad for less than four hours' fishing in a water temperature of 49 degrees F. and an air temperature around freezing. But I had to pay for that. The day after heavy rain came in, and the river rose. It was up and down every day for the next six weeks. At the very end of January the wind swung into the east, the temperature plunged below zero and conditions could only be described as Arctic. Perfect! While still retaining some colour the Trent dropped rapidly, due to the excess water being frozen into the ground. It actually warmed up, too, going above 50 degrees F. for the first time for weeks. This was due to everyone switching on the heaters, which puts the power stations on full load, which in turn means that they pump out more warm water.

My biggest problem was the east wind, for in the swim I was fishing it was straight in my face, and so mind-numbingly cold I had to erect the brolly and sit with my back to the river. This made it difficult to watch the rod tops for those telltale chub pulls, so I limited my stay to little more than two hours per trip. I used a variety of boilies over the next three weeks, during which time I fished 10 times and caught 11 carp. On February 8 another monster snowfall blanketed the country, but this time it froze on the ground and did not affect the river much at all. It did give me the chance to photograph a lovely common of 14lbs with a background of snow, something I had always wanted to do. That period was brilliant for me, as I also had my first 6lb chub, and the weekend piking trips produced fish of 25.8 and 25.10 at my favourite gravel pit.

February 5 provided the highlight of the winter. I had two rods cast out by 6 p.m. and rapidly retired behind the brolly. The facing easterly was as bitter as I had ever known it, and the following day's papers said the wind chill factor took the temperature down to minus 15 degrees C., just off the scale in Fahrenheit! Even my eyebrows froze up.

At 7 p.m., just into full darkness, a cheese flavoured boilie gave me a spirited common of about 6lbs. At 7.15 a meat-based boilie produced a steady take which I instinctively knew would be a big fish. On feeling the hook it powered away heavily downstream for perhaps 50 yards, before it turned and just hung in the mid-river current. Without the shelter of the brolly the icy blast was indescribable. My eyes watered, my face went dead, with that peculiar tight feeling, and worst of all my fingers started to go numb. The carp, with a water temperature of 53 degrees F. had no such problems. It made powerful runs up and down the river, and as I had hooked it on one of my 1.75lb TC soft-actioned carbons the rod was bent so far round throughout the battle that its 12ft length was effectively reduced by half.

All I could do was hang on grimly, fighting the growing numbness in my fingers, and hope and pray that the fish would not find a snag. After

The big common, now weighing 28lb 4oz, and still scale perfect.

what seemed an age the carp's runs got shorter and shorter, and I actually began to think I might win the battle, so I grabbed the landing net and dropped it in the water at my feet. Almost with surprise I noted that I had an enormously long shape wallowing off the rod end, so I rapidly grasped the net and slid it under the huge expanse of what I could see, even in the dark, was a common carp. Then disaster! In my haste I had dropped the net in the water with the mesh wrapped around its own 3ft arms. As I lifted it under the fish it was more like a tightly stretched platform than a net into which the fish could sink. Instead of doing that the carp slid back into the water tail first, and celebrated with another scorching run which almost tore the rod from my hand. Desperately trying to unravel the net with my free hand I waited fatalistically for the slack line which would signal yet another lost fight. Worse still, the wet net had finished off my left hand. The Arctic wind had turned it into what felt like a fingerless fist, and I could only turn the reel handle in a curious, stiff-wristed fashion. In addition my face was turning into a sheet of glass.

Incredibly, though, it was the fish which had had enough. I cranked it straight back to the bank and into the landing net without further protest. Parting the mesh I found myself looking at the big common, for the third time that season, at its best weight of 28lbs 4oz. It was easily recognisable by the missing top section of its tail fin - the only flaw in an otherwise immaculate carp. Look at the photograph. It is one of the most splendid commons you are ever likely to see, and what marvellous ammunition to use against the antis. That fish had been caught at least three times in seven months, weighed, photographed and returned by myself on each occasion, yet it was still scale perfect and putting on weight. Not much evidence of a cruel sport, is there?

The fight had lasted 15 minutes, and my total fishing time was 90 minutes. If you get everything right, and it all comes together, that is all the time you need. I did not continue to fish. I felt I'd had a slice of good luck this time, and was unlikely to better such a catch. So it proved, and half a dozen low double commons later the season ran out on me.

1991

I could not complain about 1990, despite the big disaster. That 30lb target had loomed suddenly nearer, and I could not wait to start again in June, 1991. First, however, there were tackle improvements to make. I had felt badly under-powered on the 28lb common, and totally inadequate when I lost the monster. When the 16th came around again I was kitted out with two 2lb test Armalite carbons, and the new Terry Eustace Big Game line. Rated at 12lb, it actually breaks at 15/16lb after being knotted and soaked for 10 hours. The business end was the reliable Super Silk and Partridge Z17 eyed hooks. A word about these hooks. All others tend to open out under a heavy pull, but with Z17s the hook is only driven in deeper as more pressure is put on. It is a very unusual shape (see Fig 32, page 127), but I have never used a better hook. I have not experienced any of the problems that bent hooks are said to be causing with some stillwater carp. My confidence in my tackle, my presentation and my baits was sky high. Let me at 'em!

Of course, in comes the wobbler factor, and June 1991 was the coldest and wettest since records began. With the Trent rising fast, cold and dirty my 41st fishing season started on June 17th, breaking a lifetime's tradition of midnight starts on the 15th/16th. I still blanked, as I did on the 18th and 19th, but the 21st was a different matter. I had decided to try a new area for a change, for with the higher levels my regular swims were pushing through a bit.

During the close season I had restricted my bait-making a little, this time making only nine different boilie mixes, plus, of course, the flavoured maize. At 9.15 p.m. one of my new baits was taken. By now I knew that a slowly bleeping Optonic signalled a big fish, as opposed to the continuous scream caused by the small commons. This carp went away on the usual powerful run, but for the first time I felt in full control, right from the start. Even though the fish made several determined efforts to reach a nearby snag my tackle was more than equal to the task, and I piled on the pressure relentlessly. Within 10 minutes it was in the net, and I knew straight away it would go 25lbs. It turned out to be a remarkably accurate guess, for it weighed 25lb 2oz, a beautiful mirror carp. Not a bad first fish of the season, for an expenditure of six boilies on the stringer and one on the hook.

An hour later two lads came down to night fish, so I decided to leave them to it. Before I had even packed up they had fired 200 to 300 boilies into the swim, so I did not bother to tell them about my fish. I learned later that they had two small commons in a 15 hour session with four rods. I returned to the swim three days after and took commons of 10.4 and 11.4, on Gorgonzola flavoured maize, and again the two lads turned up. They were not fishing; just baiting up the swim ready for the weekend. They had over 1000 boilies with them, and I realised it was time to move. Baiting on that scale pulls in all the small carp in the area, not to mention hordes of chub, and the chances of contacting that cruising monster become quite remote.

I roamed up and down the river, trying swims here and there, working through my range of boilies and still trying different flavours on the maize. Yes, I know there are peanuts, maples, tigers and a whole host of other particles, but most of them need cooking, which takes time and preparation. Maize works well enough just soaked. In any case seeds are but a simple carrier to me, a vehicle for my ever-changing flavour experiments, much as bread paste was in the feeder days. One day, perhaps, a blend of oil, spice, sweetener and aminos, for example, will prove to be the bait to end all baits.

Meanwhile I fished around and picked up the odd carp, mostly in the 9 to 12lb class and topped by a nice common of 15.8. There were anglers on the river catching more carp than me by using the mass bait/long stay approach. They put more time in on one weekend than I did in a fortnight, without ever getting near to a really big fish. I was certain that sooner or later my minimum feed tactics would pay off, so I persevered, though that summer's fishing was far poorer than the previous one, and the autumn was even worse. Even though I was fishing the clean part of the Trent I began to suspect increased pollution, for we were then well into the "relaxed consent" period which, loosely translated, meant that certain people could pollute the river legally, instead of illegally. The promise was that we would have cleaner rivers in the end, but since those promises were made by politicians there is a 50/50 chance that they are valueless.

Maybe low flows had something to do with it, but it was in this generally slow period, on August 14th, that my quest was nearly

A beautiful mirror weighing 25lb 2oz - not a bad start to the season.

29lb 4oz – 12oz short of the ultimate target.

completed, just under two years after it first began. From 6 p.m. to 10.15 p.m. the water seemed dead, and I had already decided to be away at 10.30 p.m. Just into full dark the now familiar slow bleeping of the Optonic commenced, and as I tightened into the fish it moved off downstream with immense power. I let it go, as there was a large snag some 50 yards upstream, but that fish knew all about it. Within seconds it had turned and was forging relentlessly upstream towards the obstruction. Time to test the new tackle. As the carp came level I really leaned into it, to try and swing it off course. It had no effect and the fish moved ponderously towards its goal, the line ticking remorselessly off the spool.

I had no alternative but to clamp down completely. I gave it everything I had, and slowly the fish lost speed until it was at a standstill. Both carp and angler were frozen into immobility for a few brief seconds. Suddenly the carp gave up, turning and going with speed down the river again. I was thankful to let it go. Over the next 15 minutes it made a further six attempts to get past me and towards that snag, but each time it was stopped by maximum pressure from the tackle. Not once did I feel I was going to lose it. Eventually the fish was finished, and wallowing heavily at the rod end, but I was in for a surprise of a different kind this time. As it went into the net I caught a glimpse of a ragged tail lobe and, yes, I was once again looking at the big common. I knew it was heavier, and the scales this time said 29.4 - so near to my target.

So where does all this leave me? I have now caught this fish twice, and seen it caught twice more. It is even conceivable that I will catch it again, maybe at 30lb plus. Will that be the end of my quest? No, it has to be a different fish, preferably a mirror, for the Trent reverses the normal stillwater preferences. Commons are the norm; mirrors the rarities. I wonder which variety the monster was.

Now and again I dream of fighting that fish once more, this time on more equal terms (or would it see off my revised tackle too?). How big was it, for heaven's sake? Word is that the Trent record is now 35lbs from the tidal river, but in my heart of hearts I simply cannot believe the fish I fought and lost was only a few pounds bigger than the 29.4 common. It was very possibly a big 30, but unless I catch it with my hook still in it, which is extremely unlikely, I will never know the truth.

These dreams, these mysteries, triumphs and disappointments, however, are the very essence of angling. It is better to have fought and lost, than never to have fought at all!

SUMMING UP

by Colin Dyson

For those already sold on the idea of flavoured baits the foregoing chapters will have been a real education. There are some, however, who may have to suspend their disbelief, or who may attribute Archie Braddock's successes to other factors. I tended towards that belief myself until I studied what he had to say for long enough, and began to try some of his ideas.

He has mentioned some of my results, but not all, and he did not know that I had been trying various things myself, long before he ever brought up the subject with me. I could never give it the sustained field-testing that he has, simply because I live too far away from decent venues to go as often as he does, and I also tend to enjoy a greater variety of fishing. To get as far as Archie has requires lengthy dedication to just one method.

I never learned enough to be adamant about anything, but various things I did discover all tend to support what he has to say. One reason why Archie bags up as often as he does is that he fishes the right places at the right time. Fishing when the fish feed best, in the last hour or so of daylight and into the dark, as he usually does, one expects to catch more fish than is possible in match hours. What the more inexperienced readers should realise, therefore, is that improved and enhanced baits cannot in themselves create bonanza catches.

I do not think Archie would claim that, but what he would say is that his approach will improve the results at any given time. His own catches in very unfavourable winter conditions bear that out, and I have had experiences which support the case. Indeed I went out of my way to fish at the worst possible time for bream on a shallow club lake, turning up several times at mid-day in a heatwave. Each time I started with conventional maggot fishing, and failed to get a bite. Then I switched to two of the more simple paste baits Archie has written about - cheese-flavoured bread paste and his sausage meat/Weetabix/Bovril recipe. I also used cheese-flavoured groundbait.

The sausage meat I initially lobbed out on strong tackle, hoping for a carp, and the float was dithering all the time I was failing to catch on maggot, on the other rod. It was obvious that something was pecking away at the big ball of bait, and when I reeled it in it had all but gone. I put a small piece on an 18 hook and caught a bream. Two more took the meat, but back on maggot I was biteless again. I then tried the cheese paste (artificial, not natural cheese) and caught six more.

The baits caught when the fish didn't really want to feed. It was blazing hot, with no wind, but in the last two hours before dark they went silly. They were not big bream, for the lake does not hold any, but they were mostly the better bream of 1lb 4oz to 2lb. The main problem, even in the busy spell, was hitting the bites. Pole fishing with

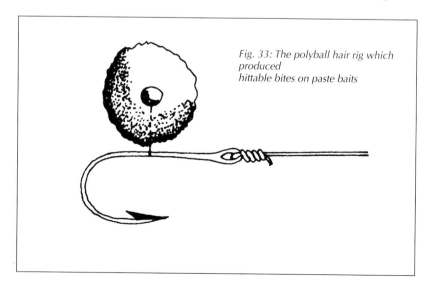

Fig. 33: The polyball hair rig which produced
hittable bites on paste baits

elastic, which has to be used because there are carp and tench as well as bream, is not as effective with paste baits when the hook is buried. I missed more than I hit. Before the next trip I did a number of experiments at home with little polyballs superglued to a short hair rig (Fig.33).In reality it was a thread of silk, superglued to the shank of the hook, sizes 18 and 16. When the paste was moulded round the polyball it either floated off the bottom or had virtually neutral buoyancy. The hair was very short, and the hook, totally exposed, was tight up against the paste. I hoped the bream would take it right in, even with a half-hearted suck, and that seemed to be the case. The pattern, on another hot day, repeated itself, only this time I hit nearly every bite. On the third trip the place was bang off form, and I caught only three fish, all on cheese paste.

I had a few sessions on the tidal Trent which proved very difficult. Nobody was catching anything, probably because the river was stale after weeks without rain. Again I tried maggot, attracting bites from just a few bits of tin, but the sausage paste produced six nice hybrids.

Flavoured dead maggots? Yes, I tried them on the bream lake, and caught very well on them. It felt very strange using them, and despite what Archie had said I had no confidence at all until the float dipped just a few seconds after the first cast. On very soft-bottomed stillwaters I reckon this approach could be a real winner, though I must emphasise something Archie mentioned. Dead maggots go off very quickly when they thaw out, and it might be best to keep them in a cool box, or one of the insulated bags which are now available to keep boilies in good condition.

I was also very keen to try dead maggots on the Trent, and got the opportunity when I went with Archie to take a few pictures for this book. Fate decreed that the river was on the rise after months of stagnation, and Archie had been fishing for an hour or so before I got there. He had been catching smallish bream, roach and gudgeon, and after a while I took over his rod. The maggots were treated with Maple Cream, and smelled so strongly I suspected that they had been dosed with more than the "regulation" 5ml per pint.

Not really, according to Archie, who came out with something he either forget to include in the book or had learned since he wrote the relevant section. He had given them 5ml per pint, and had left them to work in it for 24 hours. Immediately before freezing them up he had sprayed them with just a bit more of the flavour .

Carp anglers discovered that neutral boilies sprayed with a flavour take that flavour in when they thaw out. There is an argument that maggots do not take in flavours, and that it all washes away as soon as they hit the water. The contrary view that they take in at least some of it is based on what we know some bait breeders do to freshen and liven up old maggots. They add water mixed with blood, and the maggots eat it and plump out. Also, if you try, and fail, to get maggots to take a dye you will find that the feed spot inside the maggot shows the colour, even if their skin does not.

They must, therefore, take in at least some of what is given to them, and dead maggots probably take a flavour better than live ones. Their skins are certainly a great deal softer when they are dead, and that half gallon of Maple Cream maggots smelled much more than any live maggots I have treated at 5ml to a pint! The session which followed was very interesting, and it knocked a hole in the idea that the smell just washes off.

I carried on getting a bite every cast from small fish, but since we were downstream fishing for bream, in a way which was not particularly sensitive for smaller fish, I missed most of them. With three maggots on a 14 that was par for the course, but I did land five different species and, eventually, a bream of nearly 3lb.

Every cast produced bites which reduced the maggots to skins, the first one coming within seconds of the feeder hitting bottom. If it wasn't a strong pull I did not strike, waiting for maggot no. 2 to be dealt with. If again there was no strong pull I just left it, striking instantly at the third movement of the tip. Every now and again, however, I tried dead maggots which had been treated with a different flavour (cheese), and there were no pulls at all. Back on Maple Cream I was back in business each time, and that could not have happened if the flavour was washing out, unless you believe in monumental coincidence! They wanted Maple Cream; they did not want cheese. In Archie's view live, untreated maggots would not have produced many bites at all, in those conditions.

The dead maggots were (a) visible and (b) effective. The little fish were giving them quite a tweak, and anything capable of taking three on a 14 in one go was hooked, for they gave steadier pulls which were easy to strike. The bream took it round and held it there, a supremely confident bite. Had we stayed on into the dark we would have bagged up, I think, but both of us had to go.

The possibilities for flavoured dead maggots in matches are too obvious to mention, and I cannot understand why only the occasional specimen hunter has cottoned on to them thus far (and then only for visibility on soft bottoms). I should have picked up on it, for I can remember reading about the use of dead maggots at Redmire, many years ago - by Roger Bowskill, I seem to recall.

Further evidence that additives work can already be found in the match fishing world. A Scunthorpe match angler, using an undisclosed additive, did so well on the River Ancholme in 1989 and 1990 that he earned the ultimate accolade; his rivals were seriously talking about banning him. That is just one bit of independent evidence to support what Archie Braddock has to say. There was also the Leeds match angler who cleaned up on a special bait and put it on the market. Little has been heard of him or his product since, but that supports Archie as well. Doesn't he say, time and time again, that no single approach works everywhere, or all the time? And doesn't he stress the need for constant change? Different flavours for different times of the year? If he was wrong we would still be buying little plastic pots of fragrant pink powder, and that Leeds angler would be a millionaire!

The real biggie in Archie's book is his assertion that there is a flavour which will sort out not only the required species, but the bigger fish of a given species. His own results are proof enough for him, but I do not think he will achieve total acceptance, not in the short term anyway. Few will buy that until they actually prove it for themselves, but that is exactly what he is inviting people to do. Knowing him as I do, I doubt that he would make such a statement unless he was utterly convinced it was true, and that he could not be proved wrong..

Whether I will have the resolution to try and prove him right is debatable, but part of my early experience with flavours tends to support him. One attractor I tried for bream - it was basically Sensas Magic mixed with Tonic (vanilla powder) - was an absolutely brilliant groundbait for skimmer bream, but it never produced the better bream which inhabited the lake where I tried it most often. It attracted them into the swim, but for some reason failed to persuade them feed. At times I had the swim bulging with bream, but the only decent bream I ever caught when using that particular attractor were foulhooked! Archie would have worried away at that problem like a dog with a juicy bone, but I never got to the bottom of it. I didn't stick with it long enough. Years later I did catch the better bream there - it was the same lake which responded so well to his cheese and sausage pastes!

To deny the basic premise that flavours catch fish is to be almost Luddite. It flies in the face of all the evidence. The theory was proven beyond any doubt by the carp fishermen, though they were not the first to think of it. I once read a little booklet, produced and published in the last century, which discussed bait colours and the merits of particular herbs and powders, even down to which appealed to which species, and it wasn't new even then. It was forgotten, though, for the greater part of this century. We took little notice, and maybe even laughed when the occasional story surfaced about tench, for example, responding to the smell and taste of tar.

Now we do not bat an eye when carp anglers catch on after-shave, yet many are still reluctant to accept that species other than carp respond in similar ways, even when people actually prove it. To try the same approach on tench was the logical next step, and it worked. Angler/writers such as Len Arbery and Alan Beat were soon into special baits for tench, and filed away somewhere I have one of Alan's most effective recipes. It dates back almost a decade, but I have yet to try it. Specials and mini-boilies are now the standard approach for tench, I am sad to say, though most of the sadness stems from the fact that the new baits go hand in hand with bolt rigs and horizon casting. People can do as they wish, but I will never, ever, fish for tench that way. As far as that species is concerned I am a misty dawn float man.

For some reason the new bait trend did not spread naturally from carp and tench to all the other species, though match anglers have dabbled at it, mainly via the continental groundbaits. Maggot additives from Daiwa, which they claim to be more effective in giving the bait a smell which survives immersion in water, are relatively new, but I still smile when I recall Roy Marlow explaining them to me at a trade show. Roy is nobody's fool. In fact I think I can recall him writing that fruity flavours were more effective in the warmer months before Archie Braddock told me the same thing.

Roy knew he was treading on the edges of the unknown when Daiwa launched the additives. He admitted that the quantities to use were a matter for experiment and that the labelling might be wrong. He had, for example, caught a lot of bream on the one which was supposed to catch carp! No matter; the point is they work, and it is up to the angler to sort out the fine detail.

It certainly adds a new dimension to a fascinating pastime, and I agree with Archie that it is a passport to better catches. Be prepared for the occasional failure, though. Archie will not thank me for saying so, but when I read his accounts of pike taking maggots flavoured with certain additives the penny dropped. I remembered a couple of

Colin Dyson, with one of the pike which decided to take an unflavoured bait!

occasions when he came to my gravel pit with deadbaits which smelled like a fish market at the end of a hot day. I did not ask, and he did not tell, but I caught 20-pounders and other big fish both days, and he caught nothing at all!

However good those additives were on maggots in summer, my pike were not at all impressed in winter! If there is an answer, though, he will find it! As I indicated in the introduction, he is a difficult man to fish with. You know that one day he is going to turn up and empty the place!

Other popular books by

PUBLICATIONS

My Way With the Pole by Tom Pickering
Comprehensive guide to pole fishing
by an England international and
former World Champion angler (Hardback **£12.95**, softback **£9.95**)

Modern Match Fishing by Dave King
A must for ambitious matchmen, with a
foreword by Ken Giles (Softback **£7.95**)

The Modern Coarse Angler by Dave King
A wealth of basic advice and instruction (Softback **£7.95**)

Also available via Pisces Angling Publications

A Fishery of Your Own by Barrie Rickards and Ken Whiting
A superb guide to fisheries management (Hardback **£9.95**)

Pike Anglers' Manual by Barrie Rickards and Martin Gay
Basic and advanced techniques (Softback **£4.95**)

Pisces Angling Publications, PO Box 657, Sheffield S10 1AT